HERBS Herbs Herbs

Over 200 mouth watering dishes for every season, using nature's supreme ingredients

HERBS Herbs *Herbs*

Over 200 mouth watering dishes for every season, using nature's supreme ingredients

Edited by Lyn Coutts

CHARTWELL
BOOKS, INC.

A QUINTET BOOK

Published by Chartwell Books
A division of Book Sales, Inc.
114, Northfield Avenue
Edison, New Jersey 08837

This edtition produced for sale in the U.S.A, its
territories and dependencies only.

ISBN 0-7858-0924-4

This book was designed and produced by
Quintet Publishing Limited
6 Blundell Street
London N7 9BH

Creative Director: Richard Dewing
Art Director: Lucy Parissi
Design: Siân Keogh
Project Editor: Toria Leitch
Editor: Lyn Coutts
Illustrator: Shona Cameron

Material in this book previously appeared in: *Natural Cooking*,
Elizabeth Cornish; *Salads*, Sue Mullin; *Dressings and Marinades*,
Hilaire Walden; *Lebanese Cooking*, Susan Ward; *Sauces and Salsas
Cookbook*, Silvana Franco; *The encyclopedia of Homemade Dips*,
Dawn Stock; *The Soy Sauce Cookbook*, Jenny Stacey and Maureen
Keller; *Portuguese Cooking*, Hilaire Walden; *Vegetarian Pasta
Cookbook*, Sarah Maxwell; *Creative Cooking with Spices*, Jane
Walker; *Pickles, Relishes and Chutneys*, Gail Duff.

Typeset in Great Britain by
Central Southern Typesetters, Eastbourne
Manufactured in Hong Kong by
Regent Publishing Services Ltd
Printed in China by
Leefung-Asco Printers Trading Limited

CONTENTS

INTRODUCTION

For many years herbs, both fresh and dried, were relegated to supporting roles in cooking. As garnishes, they were hastily scattered over a dish to make it look presentable; or as an ingredient, they were often added as an ill-considered afterthought. But herbs now have starring roles; restaurant menus rarely fail to list the herbs used in a dish, and the makers of ready-made meals know that if there is no herb in the name, the product will not move off the shelf. Because of this top billing, it is appropriate that we learn how to store and use herbs so as to extract their full flavors.

There is nothing new about this. Herbs, after all, are plants of great antiquity going back to the earliest civilizations. There are records of their uses and techniques of cultivation in ancient Egypt, Persia, Arabia, Greece, China, and India. The Chinese compiled a list of 365 herbs by 2700 BC. Both literally and metaphysically, herbs have their roots in our collective past.

Herbs have a magical and mystical hold over traditions in many cultures. The ancient Romans believed that a wreath of bay leaves would protect the household from lightning strikes, and the ancient Greeks burned thyme as an offering to their gods. Even in modern Greece, a wreath of herbs is often hung on the front door to absorb evil influences that could otherwise spell doom for the family.

Herbal medicine is once again being given the respect in Western cultures that it deserves. Many of us will now opt for a herbal remedy or a calming herbal tea before we reach for the medicine chest. It has been suggested that medicinal preparations—mostly based on herbs—were a by-product of cooking. All herbs have medicinal qualities, some providing the active ingredients in modern pharmaceutical compounds.

Our current affair with herbs—and long may it continue and strengthen—is comprehensive. We bathe in herbs, wash our hair with herbed shampoos, anoint wounds with herbal liniments, and last, but not least, we eat them and we are all the better for it. It seems only natural then that the nutritional benefits of many herbs should be recognized. Parsley, for example, is brimming with vitamins A, B, and C, and iron; and a handful of parsley, chewed, will also sweeten the breath.

Aiding and abetting the surge in herb cooking is the easy availability of fresh herbs—parsley, basil, dill, cilantro, and mint are on the supermarket shelves throughout the summer and beyond—and the introduction of herbs and seasonings from China, Japan, South-east Asia, the Mediterranean, and the Middle East. Herb flavors that were once considered exotic are now well on their way to becoming standard in home cooking. Cilantro, which graces almost every Thai dish, was until recently one such exotic herb.

Because of the universal nature of herbs, this book includes recipes from Portugal, Lebanon, India, Thailand, China, Italy, Greece, France, the Balkans, Mexico, South America, North America, and Russia. Though the recipes are very different, each offering the opportunity to savor varied tastes, the unifying theme is herbs. Each recipe unwraps a herb's secrets, so that their wonderful—and sometimes challenging—flavors, textures, colors, and aromas are revealed. The types of dishes range from the wholesome to the indulgent, simple and basic to the complex and sophisticated. There are recipes for vegetarians, and for parties, family meals, breakfasts and brunches, picnics, suppers, and formal dinners.

PERFECT PARTNERS

Certain herbs and foods go together like Gable and Leigh, Astaire and Rogers. They combine in exciting relationships, or meld in perfect harmony. Some of these partnerships are well-established in cooking: chives with potatoes or eggs; dill with fish or cucumbers; tarragon with chicken; basil and tomatoes; rosemary and lamb; bay leaf with stews and even custard. Indeed, without the frisson of sage and veal, there is nothing "jump in the mouth" about the Italian dish, saltimbocca.

Some starring herb partnerships include: thyme, marjoram, and sage; and basil and oregano. Parsley goes with just about everything, and even seems to enhance the flavor of the herbs in its company.

Do not be bound by these relationships, however, experiment and develop your own specialties using the recipes in this book as a base. Likewise, the measurements, timings, and temperatures suggested in this book are not written on tablets of stone. It is far better to employ your own good judgment and sensitive palate. The only way to really tell if the flavors of a dish are as you want them is to taste as you cook. Products vary from brand to brand, and even the flavor of herbs varies from season to season. Many herbs are at their prime for only

HERBS WORK PARTICULARLY WELL IN DRESSINGS AND MARINADES

short periods, therefore it may be necessary to increase or even decrease the quantity of herbs used in a particular recipe. The exception to this is parsley, which retains a consistent flavor throughout the year.

When creativity gets the better of you and you venture alone to try new herb combinations, bear in mind that lovage, oregano, marjoram, hyssop, bay, sage, thyme, and rosemary are regarded as strongly pungent and flavorful herbs, so use judiciously. Note that recipes using uncooked eggs should not be consumed by people at risk, such as those with weak immune systems and pregnant women.

GRILLED SARDINES WITH ROSEMARY

GROWING HERBS

Recall how you savor the aroma of herbs in dishes, then imagine enjoying those aromas every time you walked into your garden or kitchen. Herbs will not only add sparkle and zest to your cooking, but they will also help to purify and sweeten your environment.

Easy herbs to grow indoors in pots on windowsills are: thyme, rosemary, marjoram, parsley, and chives. Even mint is best confined to a pot. Plant herbs in a good-quality potting mix into fair-sized pots with adequate drainage holes. It may be necessary to use a liquid fertilizer to maintain the nutrients in the potting mix to encourage good growth. Site the pots in a sunny, warm position, and water frequently.

In the garden, depending on location and aspect, a traditional herbal garden is possible. But if space is limited, make sure you plant at least some of the following: bay, basil, rosemary, lemongrass, parsley, marjoram, thyme, and oregano.

The best time to harvest fresh herbs is as soon before cooking as possible, or in the morning before they are warmed by the heat of the sun. Sever the sprigs or stems with scissors so that the leaves are not bruised. Store them until needed as described in the next section. Harvest herbs for drying just as they begin to flower to take advantage of their full flavor at this time. Gather them on a dry day, or after the dew has dried.

PREPARING AND STORING HERBS

Rinse herbs in cold water and remove any discolored leaves. Shake or pat with paper towels to dry before cutting with a sharp knife, or tearing by hand as for basil, on a chopping board.

To store herbs for later use, keep the stems intact and wash gently in cold water so as not to bruise the leaves or break the stems. Then dry the herbs in a salad basket, or pat dry with paper towels. To keep herbs in prime condition, place them in a clean polythene bag with sheets of moist paper towel, seal the bag and store in the crisper or vegetable compartment of a refrigerator. It may be necessary to replace the paper towels with freshly moistened ones.

Alternatively, place the herbs in a glass jar, their stems in water, and cover with a polythene bag. Store in a refrigerator. Occasionally shake the jar and top up with fresh water.

You can freeze any leftover small bunches of green herbs, such as mint or chives, by washing and drying them, wrapping them in aluminum foil or plastic wrap, and placing them in the freezer where they will stay flavorful for about two months. Use these frozen herbs for cooking only, though, because while freezing doesn't ruin the flavor, it causes the leaves to go limp.

USING AND STORING DRIED HERBS

Dried herbs are used direct from their containers. The flavor of dried herbs is more concentrated than fresh ones, so substitute a teaspoon of dried herb for a tablespoon of fresh. Make sure that you store dried herbs away from heat in a cool, dimly lit place in sealed containers.

DRYING HERBS

You can successfully dry your own herbs by tying the stems together in small bunches and hanging them upside down and out of direct sunlight in a closet, attic, or kitchen. When the herbs are dry (allow about two weeks), place them on a paper towel and remove the leaves from the stems. Discard the stems and then rub the leaves through a fine-mesh strainer to remove any stray bits of stem.

Air-drying herbs has two drawbacks. In the city, polluted air can make air-drying seem less than satisfactory; and it is said that the quicker the herbs are dried, the better their flavor will be. For these reasons you may prefer to dry herbs in an oven. To do this, place the herbs in a single layer on a baking sheet lined with either aluminum foil or paper towels, and set the oven to its lowest temperature. Leave the herbs in the oven for twelve hours, or until the leaves are brittle. Remove from the oven, allow the herbs to cool, and then strip the leaves from the stems. Store the dried herbs as described above.

WHEN TO ADD HERBS

Bouquet garni and selected herbs are best added to long-cooking foods during the final 60 minutes of cooking. Add fresh herbs (an exception is basil) to quickly-cooked foods, like omelets or pasta sauces, along with the other ingredients. Basil should be mixed in toward the end of cooking. Dried herbs should be soaked in a little milk before being added. Add mint to green peas and potato dishes at the start of cooking, then add a few more sprigs at the end.

HERBS

BASIL The best and most flavorful variety is grown in the Mediterranean. Those grown elsewhere, even in its native India, are just never as fragrant. The small leaf variety has a stronger flavor than the large leaf basil. Basil has many uses and can be added liberally to dishes, but its most famous incarnation is in pesto sauce. Aficionados call it the tomato herb because of its affinity with this fruit. Dried basil is not a satisfactory substitute for fresh.

BAY Bay is not strictly a herb, it is an evergreen perennial, and its leaves can be used dried or fresh. Remove the bay leaf from the dish at the end of the cooking. Though sometimes known as laurel, bay is not to be confused with poisonous varieties of laurel.

BOUQUET GARNI This seasoning, bound in a cheesecloth bag, consists of parsley, thyme, and bay leaf. Add it to soups, and stews.

CILANTRO Also known as Chinese parsley or coriander, it resembles flat-leaf parsley, but its pungent citrus-like flavor gives it a distinctive character. It looks wonderful as garnish, and the flavor will permeate any dish. When buying cilantro, look for vigorous, deep green leaves; avoid bunches or potted cilantro with limp or yellow leaves.

CHIVES It seems a pity to buy chives, when they are so easily grown in the garden or in a small pot on a sunny windowsill, and then freshly harvested. Their oniony taste makes them ideal as a garnish, to flavor sauces and cooked dishes, and to add bite to salads. The purple blossom can be eaten. Chinese chives, which have larger stems, taste of garlic.

DILL Its distinctive feathery leaves and heavenly caraway flavor and aroma make this a favorite herb in Greek, Turkish, and Russian cooking, but it is best known in dill pickles. Use it in salads, egg dishes, and cooked vegetables, or as a garnish and flavoring for fish dishes.

FINES HERBES This is a mixture of chopped aromatic herbs such as parsley, chervil, tarragon, and chives, combined in various proportions to suit the dish. It can be used to flavor sauces, cream cheese, meat, sautéed vegetables, and omelets.

HERBES DE PROVENCE This refers to those herbs that have basked in the long hours of sunshine and sunk their roots into the fine soil of the Provence region of France. Included are thyme, marjoram, tarragon, juniper, lavender, bay, rosemary, and fennel. Great for broiled dishes.

MARJORAM This herb can be used in almost any meat dish—meat loaf, stews, liver dishes, and sausages—but some fish dishes are also enhanced by its flavor. Count among these: baked fish, salmon cakes, and creamed shellfish. Marjoram complements mushroom dishes, green beans and peas, potato dishes, Brussels sprouts, eggplants, asparagus, carrots, spinach, and zucchini. It can even liven up a coleslaw.

MINT Applemint, orange mint, and Bowles mint are varieties of mint, but it is spearmint that finds its way to the dinner table. It is used as a garnish, or to flavor sauces, relishes, and stuffings. It complements many desserts and fruit salads. Add it to lentil dishes, or to potato salads dressed with mayonnaise for a tasty change. Mint is also used to flavor drinks.

OREGANO Also known as wild marjoram, this peppery-flavored herb grows wild over the hills of Italy and Greece. It is a natural partner for cheese, tomatoes, beans, and eggplant dishes. If using dried, use the Greek variety—called *rigani*.

PARSLEY Curly-leaf parsley is slowly being overtaken in the popularity stakes by its Italian relative, flat-leaf parsley. Despite its strong flavor, this herb can be used in generous quantities, and added to many dishes as you would salt. As an extra special touch, fry curly-leaf parsley as an accompaniment to a fish dish. Use only the fresh herb, the dried herb is tasteless.

ROSEMARY A herb that is easy to grow and harvest, and gives year-round pleasure in the garden. Rosemary has a special affinity with roasted or broiled chicken and lamb. Use judiciously fresh, and avoid dried rosemary as it can have an unpleasant taste.

TARRAGON Referred to by the French as the "king of herbs," tarragon leaves (do not use the stem) make a welcome addition to salads, cooked dishes, and sauces such as Béarnaise and Hollandaise. If given a choice, use the more flavorful French rather than Russian tarragon.

THYME One of the best known and popular herbs, use it to flavor stews, soups, roast meat dishes, stuffings for poultry, and to season tomatoes, potatoes, zucchini, eggplant, and bell peppers. It partners well with wine, especially in slow-cooked dishes. Preserved olives taste all the better with the addition of thyme. Its strong, sharp taste can overpower some dishes, so you may prefer to use the more subtle lemon thyme.

Soups, Spreads, & Dips

BORSCHT

Serves 6

A Russian and Polish specialty, strongly flavored with beets and other vegetables.

INGREDIENTS

2 large onions

3 large beets

3 large carrots

2 parsnips

4 stalks celery

3 Tbsp tomato paste

4 large tomatoes

½ small white cabbage, shredded

1 Tbsp honey

1 Tbsp lemon juice

salt and freshly ground black pepper

handful of chopped parsley

a little all-purpose flour

*sour cream or unsweetened yogurt,
to serve*

Cut onions, beets, carrots, parsnips, and celery into matchsticks. Then bring a large pan of salted water to a boil, add the tomato paste and the vegetables and simmer them for 30 minutes or so, or until tender.

Skin the tomatoes, remove the seeds, and chop. Add to the pan with the cabbage, honey, lemon juice, and seasoning. Simmer for 5 minutes, then throw in a handful of chopped parsley. Check seasoning.

If necessary, thicken the soup with a blend of flour and sour cream. The soup is best made the day before eating. Serve chilled or reheat and serve with a bowl of sour cream or yogurt.

SUN-DRIED TOMATO DRESSING

Makes about 1½ cups

**This naturally sweet dressing is excellent when served on strong-flavored greens,
such as aragula and radicchio, or drizzled over pasta or crostini.**

INGREDIENTS

12 sun-dried tomatoes, soaked in water
until plump, then drained

2 garlic cloves

1 tsp dried oregano

1 Tbsp tomato paste

6 Tbsp balsamic vinegar

salt and freshly ground black pepper

½ cup olive oil

Place the tomatoes, garlic, oregano, tomato paste, and vinegar in a blender or food processor and purée. Add salt and pepper to taste. With the machine running, gradually add the oil in a steady stream until well combined. The dressing will keep for about 3 days, covered, in the refrigerator.

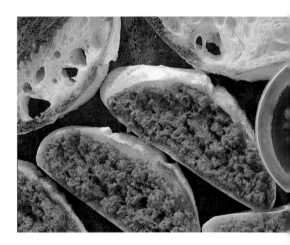

BEAN SOUP

Serves 4–6

A hearty, wholesome, and filling soup that is a meal in itself served with crusty bread.

INGREDIENTS

1 cup navy beans

1–2 Tbsp oil

1 onion, chopped

1 garlic clove, chopped

2 carrots, chopped

2 stalks celery, chopped

2 medium tomatoes, peeled
and chopped

1 slice lemon

soy sauce

salt and freshly ground black pepper

chopped parsley for garnish

Soak the navy beans in water overnight. Then bring them to a boil in a large pan of water (about 5 cups or so) and simmer until the beans are tender.

Meanwhile, heat the oil in a skillet and cook the onion and garlic until soft. Add carrots, celery, and tomatoes in that order, stirring all the while.

Tip vegetables into the pan with the cooked beans. Add the lemon and soy sauce. Taste and adjust seasoning. Heat through and serve sprinkled with the parsley.

SALMON PATE

Serves 4

This is a quickly prepared, yet delicious appetizer. Once the fish is cooked, all the ingredients are simply blended in a food processor. Canned, rather than fresh, salmon can be used.

INGREDIENTS

8 oz salmon fillet

½ cup cream cheese

1 Tbsp light soy sauce

1 Tbsp chopped fresh dill

1 Tbsp chopped fresh parsley

1 Tbsp lemon juice

1 Tbsp capers

ground black pepper

½ tsp paprika

dill sprigs and lemon slices for garnish

hot toast, to serve

Poach the salmon fillets in a large shallow pan for 8–10 minutes or until cooked through. Remove from the pan, drain, and skin the fish. Chop the fish into pieces and let cool completely.

Place the cream cheese, soy sauce, dill, parsley, lemon juice, capers, pepper, and cooked salmon in a food processor and blend for 15 seconds.

Transfer to four individual serving dishes. Sprinkle with paprika and chill in the refrigerator until required. Garnish and serve with hot toast cut into triangles.

CHIVE AND SMOKED OYSTER DIP

Makes about 1¼ cups

An indulgently creamy dip that takes only minutes to prepare.

INGREDIENTS

*two 3½-oz cans smoked oysters in oil,
well drained (you require about 6 oz
drained weight of oysters)*

2 Tbsp chopped fresh chives

⅔ cup sour cream

freshly ground black pepper

Melba toast, to serve

Reserve two oysters and a few chopped chives for garnish. Place the remaining oysters and sour cream into a blender or food processor and process for a few seconds until smooth. Turn the mixture into a bowl and stir in the chives. Season well with pepper. Cover and chill in the refrigerator until ready to use.

Transfer the dip to a serving dish, and garnish with the reserved oysters and chives. Serve with crispy Melba toast.

EGGPLANT DIP

Makes about 2 cups

**This dip combines two smoky flavors: those of the broiled eggplant and the
tahini or sesame paste.**

INGREDIENTS

2 medium eggplant, cut in half

juice of 1 lemon

2 garlic cloves, crushed

3 Tbsp tahini

½ tsp ground cumin

salt and freshly ground black pepper

*1 Tbsp chopped flat-leaf parsley, and
black olives for garnish*

Arab bread or pita, to serve

Prick the skins of the halved eggplants and lay them, flesh-side down, on a greased baking sheet. Place them under a hot broiler and broil for about 15–20 minutes, until the skins are blackened and blistered, and the flesh is soft. Remove them from the oven, plunge them into cold water, then skin thoroughly.

Chop the eggplant flesh, and put it into the bowl of a blender or food processor fitted with a metal blade. Add the lemon juice and process for a few seconds, until combined. Then add the garlic, *tahini*, cumin, and seasoning to taste. Process the mixture until it becomes a smooth purée.

Turn the purée into a bowl, cover, and chill slightly. Before serving, sprinkle over the chopped parsley and black olives. Serve with Arab bread or pita.

TOMATO AND CILANTRO SOUP

Serves 6

This is a refreshing cold summer soup that would make an excellent first course to a fish or poultry main dish. The citrus-like flavor of the cilantro perfectly complements the fruit juices in this refreshing soup.

INGREDIENTS

3 lb ripe, plump tomatoes, roughly chopped

1 small onion, chopped

¾ cup tomato juice

3 Tbsp freshly squeezed orange juice

1 Greek or Italian pickled bell pepper, seeded

¾ tsp superfine sugar

ice water

4 Tbsp finely chopped fresh cilantro

¾ cup unsweetened Greek-style yogurt

In a blender or food processor fitted with a metal blade, purée the tomatoes, onions, tomato juice, orange juice, bell pepper, and sugar.

Press the purée through a strainer, rubbing with a wooden spoon to force as much through as possible. Discard the residue, and add sufficient ice water to thin the purée to a soup-like consistency. Stir in the cilantro, cover, and chill. Pass the yogurt at the table, to allow guests to add as much as they wish.

LEMON CHICKEN SOUP

Serves 6

For the best flavor use a free-range farm chicken and only the freshest lemons and vegetables.

INGREDIENTS

4 lb chicken, cut into portions

2½ cups chicken stock

1 medium onion, chopped

2 large beefsteak tomatoes, peeled, seeded, and chopped

1 Tbsp fresh tarragon leaves

1 tsp grated lemon zest

salt and freshly ground black pepper

2 Cyprus new potatoes, peeled and chopped

8 oz okra, trimmed

½ cup canned jalapeño chiles, chopped

¾ cup frozen corn kernels

juice of 1 lemon

chopped flat-leaf parsley and paprika for garnish

In a large pan, combine chicken portions (except for the breasts), stock, onion, tomatoes, tarragon, and zest. Pour over 3 cups of water, season to taste, and bring to a boil. Reduce the heat, cover, and simmer for 20 minutes. Add the breasts and continue to cook until the breasts are just cooked through. Remove all the chicken portions from the soup with a slotted spoon and set them aside to cool.

Add the potatoes to the soup, cover and continue to simmer until the potatoes are done, about 25 minutes; add the trimmed okra after 10 minutes.

When the chicken is cool enough to handle, remove the meat from the bones, discarding the skin. Chop the meat into small pieces. Add to the soup, together with the chiles and corn kernels. Bring the soup back to a boil, reduce heat, and simmer for a further 5 minutes. Stir in the lemon juice and serve immediately, garnished with the chopped parsley and paprika to taste.

TOMATO AND BASIL DIP

Makes about 1½ cups

**Serve this dip in hollowed-out tomatoes as either a party nibble or as a colorful first course.
It can be made in advance and chilled.**

INGREDIENTS

4 beefsteak tomatoes

1 small onion, chopped

6 Tbsp chopped fresh basil

freshly ground black pepper

fresh basil leaves for garnish

*breadsticks, and strips of cucumber,
celery, and zucchini, to serve*

Slice the top off each tomato, and scoop out the flesh and seeds. Reserve the flesh and discard the seeds. Place the tomatoes upside down on a plate to drain.

Finely chop the tomato flesh and place in a non-metallic sieve. Press out any excess juice with a wooden spoon. Discard the juice.

Place half of the chopped tomato and all of the chopped onion in a blender or food processor and process until smooth. Transfer the mixture to a bowl.

Stir in the remaining chopped tomato and chopped basil, and season well. Divide the dip mixture evenly among the four hollowed-out tomatoes. Cover and broil.

Garnish with basil leaves and serve with breadsticks, and strips of cucumber, celery, and zucchini.

BREAD SOUP WITH GARLIC AND EGGS

Serves 4–6

**This is a thick, substantial, bread-based soup made from readily available and inexpensive ingredients.
Serve as an appetite-blunting first course, or as a main meal.**

INGREDIENTS

1 Spanish onion, quite finely chopped

5 garlic cloves, chopped

*1–2 fresh red chiles, seeded
and chopped*

3–4 Tbsp olive oil

½ lb firm country bread, crumbled

5 cups chicken stock, boiling

4–6 eggs, lightly beaten

handful of chopped cilantro or parsley

salt and black pepper

Cook the onion, garlic, and chiles in the oil until the onion has softened. Stir in the bread, raise the heat and cook, stirring, to lightly brown the bread.

Stir in the stock, lower the heat and stir in the eggs, cilantro or parsley, and seasoning. Then serve.

MELON SOUP

Serves 6

This ingenious two-tone cold soup—one half of each serving is yellow-orange, the other light green—is a great way of using over-ripe fruit.

INGREDIENTS

2 large Ogen melons, peeled, seeded,
and chopped

4 Tbsp lime juice

4 Tbsp superfine sugar

2 large cantaloupe melons, peeled,
seeded, and chopped

4 Tbsp lemon juice

½ cup unsweetened Greek-style yogurt

ground cinnamon and mint leaves
for garnish

In the bowl of a blender or food processor fitted with a metal blade, purée the Ogen melon, lime juice, and 2 tablespoons sugar until smooth. Pour the mixture into a pitcher, cover and chill in the refrigerator until cold.

Rinse out the bowl of the blender or processor and fill with the cantaloupe melon, lemon juice and remaining sugar. Purée until smooth. Pour into a pitcher, cover and chill until cold.

When ready to serve, position each soup bowl in front of you. Pick up both pitchers, and pour the two soups into a bowl at the same time, one on each side. Repeat with the remaining bowls.

Each soup will be two-tone; use a spoon to gently feather the edges to obtain a softer effect. Top each serving with a spoonful of yogurt. Sprinkle the yogurt with a little cinnamon and garnish with mint leaves. Serve immediately.

21

GARBANZO BEAN SPREAD

Makes about 2 cups

**A light and spicy version of the very popular Lebanese appetizer, hummus.
Spread on warmed pita bread, the citrus tang comes to the fore.**

INGREDIENTS

*15-oz can garbanzo beans in brine,
rinsed, and drained*

2 garlic cloves, crushed

2 Tbsp olive oil

1 Tbsp sunflower oil

3 Tbsp freshly squeezed lemon juice

salt and freshly ground black pepper

½ tsp cayenne pepper

¼ tsp chili powder

2 Tbsp chopped parsley

*4 oz ground lamb or beef, fried with a
little salt, pepper, and cinnamon
(optional)*

Arab bread or pita, to serve

In the bowl of a blender or food processor fitted with a metal blade, combine the garbanzo beans, garlic, and olive oil. Process until almost smooth, stopping to push down the paste from the sides of the bowl; then add the sunflower oil, lemon juice, seasoning to taste, spices, and parsley. Process until very smooth, adding a little water if you wish a thinner consistency. Scrape into a bowl and swirl the mixture decoratively.

If desired, before serving, make a small well in the center of the spread and mound in the cinnamon-fried meat. Serve with Arab bread or pita.

PEPPERY MAYONNAISE DIP

Makes about 1¼ cups

The best way to enjoy this light, almost whipped, dip is with cold, crunchy, and very fresh vegetable strips.

INGREDIENTS

1 cup mayonnaise

4 shallots, finely chopped

2 Tbsp fresh chives, finely chopped

2 Tbsp whole white peppercorns

Tabasco sauce

strips of celery, carrot, cucumber, zucchini, and blanched baby corn, to serve

Mix together the mayonnaise, shallots, and chives in a bowl. Lightly crush the peppercorns in a pestle and mortar, or place in a small plastic bag and crush lightly with a rolling pin. Stir the peppercorns into the mixture.

Add as many drops of hot Tabasco sauce as your taste prefers. Five to six drops are recommended, since the flavor matures and strengthens once the dip is chilled. Stir the mixture, then cover and chill.

Spoon the dip into a serving bowl. This dip goes particularly well served with strips of celery, carrot, cucumber, zucchini, and blanched baby sweetcorn.

BLACK OLIVE DIP

Makes about 1½ cups

There is nothing nicer than this delicious and very moreish dip. Perfect to serve with drinks and it can be made in a trice.

INGREDIENTS

14 oz canned pitted black olives in brine, drained

2 garlic cloves, minced

1 Tbsp tomato paste

1 Tbsp olive oil

1 beefsteak tomato, skinned, seeded, and chopped fine

freshly ground black pepper

fresh basil leaves for garnish

olive bread or Ciabatta, to serve

Place the olives, garlic, tomato paste, and olive oil in a blender or food processor and process for only a few seconds so that the olives retain some texture and do not form a completely smooth paste. Remove the mixture from the processor and transfer it to a bowl. Stir in the chopped tomato. Season well with black pepper. Cover the mixture and place in the in the refrigerator to chill.

Transfer the dip to a serving bowl and garnish with fresh basil leaves. Serve with wedges of olive bread or Ciabatta.

PORTUGUESE COLD SOUP

Serves 6

**Similar in taste and look to gazpacho, this version contains more bread than its Spanish equivalent.
The name gazpacho literally means "soaked bread."**

INGREDIENTS

5 well-flavored, medium tomatoes,
peeled, seeded, and finely chopped

1 red bell pepper, cored, seeded, and
finely diced

1 green bell pepper, cored, seeded,
and finely diced

½ cucumber, peeled, seeded, and
finely diced

3 garlic cloves, minced

4 Tbsp white wine vinegar

4 Tbsp olive oil

½ tsp finely chopped fresh oregano

salt and black pepper

4 slices firm, crusty bread, crusts
removed and bread cubed

3–4¼ cups iced water

Put the tomatoes, red and green bell peppers, and cucumber in a soup tureen or large bowl. Separately, whisk together the garlic, vinegar, oil, oregano, and seasoning. Pour over the tomato mixture, add the bread and stir to combine.

Stir in sufficient iced water to make a soup with a thick consistency. Chill thoroughly in the refrigerator before serving.

PINEAPPLE AND CHIVE CHEESE DIP

Makes about 1¼ cups

It is best to serve this dip fairly soon after making; on standing, the fresh pineapple exudes juice that can make the dip too moist.

INGREDIENTS

1 small, ripe pineapple

½ cup cottage cheese

2 Tbsp unsweetened yogurt

2 Tbsp chopped fresh chives

pinch of paprika

freshly ground black pepper

chopped fresh chives for garnish

crackers, and strips of celery, cucumber, and carrot, to serve

Cut the pineapple in half lengthwise. Use a sharp knife to carefully cut around the inner edge of the pineapple halves. Scoop out the flesh with a spoon. Place the empty pineapple halves upside down on a deep plate to allow excess juice to run out. Cover and chill in the refrigerator.

Cut the pineapple flesh into small chunks. Place the pieces in a non-metallic sieve over a bowl and allow any excess juice to drain.

Combine the cottage cheese with the yogurt in a bowl. Stir in the pineapple chunks, chives, and paprika. Season to taste with black pepper. Cover and chill.

Just before serving, spoon the dip into the pineapple halves and garnish with chopped chives. Serve with a selection of crackers, and chilled strips of celery, cucumber, and carrot.

SAUSAGE AND TOMATO SOUP

Serves 6

INGREDIENTS

2 slices bacon, chopped

8 oz garlic-flavored smoked sausage

8 oz morcela sausage

1 Spanish onion, halved and sliced

2 garlic cloves, minced

7 well-flavored large tomatoes, chopped

1 bay leaf

4¼ cups vegetable or chicken stock
or water

salt and black pepper

firm, crusty country bread, to serve

Cook the bacon in a saucepan until the fat has been rendered. Prick the sausages and cook with the bacon for a few minutes, then stir in the onion and garlic. Cook until soft. Add the tomatoes, bay leaf, and stock or water. Bring to a boil and simmer uncovered, for 30 minutes.

Remove the sausages and slice into rounds, return to the pan, and season. Serve with bread.

FRESH HERBED YOGURT DIP

Makes about 1¼ cups

INGREDIENTS

1 cup whole unsweetened yogurt

2 oz mixed fresh herbs (chives, parsley, oregano, thyme, and marjoram)

freshly ground black pepper

fish, meat, and vegetable kabobs, barbecued or broiled, and a selection of raw vegetable strips

Place the yogurt in a bowl. Remove any large or woody stalks from the herbs and chop the leaves fine. Add to the yogurt and mix thoroughly. Season well with black pepper. Cover and chill.

Transfer the dip to a serving bowl. Serve with fish, meat, or vegetable kabobs, and a selection of crunchy vegetable strips.

MUSHROOM AND PINE NUT DIP

Makes about 1¼ cups

Use large, flat-open mushrooms because they have a stronger flavor than the small button variety.

INGREDIENTS

4 Tbsp olive oil

9 oz large open mushrooms, finely chopped

2 oz pine nuts

8 oz canned tomatoes in tomato juice, drained and chopped

freshly ground black pepper

1 Tbsp chopped fresh parsley for garnish

crackers and crusty bread, to serve

Heat the oil in a saucepan and sauté the finely chopped mushrooms. Cook for about 10 minutes over a moderate heat so that the juices released from the mushrooms evaporate and only the olive oil and concentrated cooked mushrooms are left in the pan. Stir occasionally. Then leave the mixture in the pan to cool.

Meanwhile, place the pine nuts in a single layer on a heatproof baking sheet and place under a hot, preheated broiler. Broil for 1–2 minutes, turning occasionally, until the pine nuts turn a pale golden color. Remove from the heat and allow to cool.

Place the mushrooms and any olive oil from the pan, the tomatoes, and all but 1 tablespoon of pine nuts in a blender or food processor. Process the mixture for a few seconds until smooth. Transfer to a bowl and season. Cover and chill.

Spoon the dip into a serving bowl and sprinkle with the reserved pine nuts and chopped parsley. Serve with a selection of crackers and crusty bread.

SPROUT SOUP WITH ALMONDS

Serves 4–6

A warming soup with a subtle flavor that makes an excellent first course for a dinner party. Made up two days in advance and stored, covered, in the refrigerator, this soup can be reheated just prior to serving.

INGREDIENTS

¼ cup butter

1 garlic clove, minced

2 tsp chopped fresh rosemary

½ lb Brussels sprouts, trimmed and finely shredded

1¼ cups dried ditalini rigati (tiny, short, ridged tube pasta)

scant ½ cup toasted, slivered almonds

6½ cups vegetable broth

salt and freshly ground black pepper

4 Tbsp light cream

freshly grated Parmesan cheese, to serve

Melt the butter in a large saucepan, and sauté the garlic and rosemary for about 2 minutes. Add the Brussels sprouts and cook for a further 3–4 minutes, stirring occasionally. Add the ditalini rigati with the slivered almonds. Stir and cook for 1–2 minutes, then stir in the vegetable broth and season with salt and black pepper.

Cover the soup and simmer for about 10 minutes, stirring occasionally. Finally, stir in the light cream, then serve in individual bowls liberally sprinkled with Parmesan cheese.

VEGETABLE AND PUMPKIN SEED DIP

Makes about 1½ cups

An unusual dip in that it can be served either cold or hot. As a hot dip it is at its tastiest best when served with pumpernickel.

INGREDIENTS

1 Tbsp olive oil

1 medium onion, finely chopped

1 garlic clove, minced (optional)

1 small yellow-fleshed squash (you need about ¾ cup chopped flesh)

1 medium red bell pepper

1 tsp fresh thyme leaves

¼ cup vegetable stock or cold water

3 Tbsp pumpkin seeds

small wedges of a selection of breads (Ciabatta, tomato bread, olive bread, and pumpernickel), to serve

Heat the olive oil in a saucepan, add the onion and garlic, and sauté gently for 5 minutes, until tender but not browned. Stir occasionally.

Meanwhile, cut the squash in half and scoop out the seeds. Cut the halves into wedges and using a sharp vegetable peeler or knife, remove the squash skin. Cut the squash flesh into 1-inch cubes. Cut the bell pepper in half lengthwise, remove the seeds and dice the flesh.

Add the squash, bell pepper, and thyme to the onion and fry for 2 minutes. Add the vegetable stock or cold water, bring to a boil, cover, and simmer for 15 minutes, or until the squash is just tender. Stir occasionally. Allow to cool for at least 10 minutes before puréeing the mixture.

Lightly toast the pumpkin seeds under a hot preheated broiler—this takes only a minute, so don't leave them unattended! The pumpkin seeds begin to make a popping sound when they are ready. Remove from the broiler and leave them to cool.

Place the vegetable mixture and all but 1 tablespoon of the pumpkin seeds into a blender or food processor. Process for a few seconds on a pulse setting if possible, so that the dip retains some texture.

Transfer the dip to a serving dish and serve warm, or cover and chill before serving. Sprinkle with the remaining toasted pumpkin seeds, and serve with a selection of flavored breads such as Ciabatta, tomato, olive, and pumpernickel cut into dipping-sized wedges.

APPETIZERS & LIGHT MEALS

CRAB IN A CARRIAGE

Serves 4

The "carriage" in the recipe name refers to the crab shells in which this mixture is traditionally served.
Rinse the crabs shells before spooning in the sweet-tasting and moist crab filling.

INGREDIENTS

Piri-piri Sauce

½ red bell pepper, cored and sliced

4–5 fresh red chiles, sliced

juice of 1½ lemons

2 tsp olive oil

salt

Crab Filling

4 small fresh cooked crabs

juice of ½ lemon

¼ cup finely chopped onion

2 Tbsp olive oil

1 tsp crumbled dried thyme

2 Tbsp chopped parsley

⅔ cup mayonnaise

1–2 tsp Dijon mustard

Piri-piri sauce

salt

fresh whole wheat bread crumbs

For the Piri-piri sauce simmer the bell pepper and chiles with the lemon juice for about 15 minutes until tender. Mix to a thick paste with the oil in a blender. Season with salt. Pour into a small bottle or jar, cover, and keep cool.

For the filling twist off the legs and claws from the crab shells, crack open, and remove the meat. Remove the meat from the shells and discard the gray sac and feathery gills. Flake the meat and mix with the lemon juice. Preheat the broiler to moderate.

Fry the onion in the oil until softened. Stir in the crab meat thyme, and parsley. Remove from the heat. Stir in the mayonnaise, mustard, Piri-piri sauce, and salt to taste; the consistency should be soft.

Divide the crab mixture between the shells and sprinkle bread crumbs over the top. Place under the broiler until the mixture bubbles and is golden in color.

CHEESE AND RICE COBBLER

Serves 4

Traditionally a sweet dessert, this cobbler uses four cheeses to make the creamy sauce in which the rice is mixed. Topped with crisp bread and herb butter, it is a great dish.

INGREDIENTS

HERB BUTTER

¼ cup butter, softened

3 Tbsp chopped fresh mixed herbs

(parsley, thyme, basil, and sage)

4 slices white bread, crusts removed,

and cut into 16 triangles

RICE MIXTURE

generous 1 cup long grain white rice

2½ cups vegetable stock

2 Tbsp soy sauce

1 cup open cap mushrooms, sliced

1 Tbsp chopped fresh parsley

½ cup shredded Parmesan cheese

½ cup shredded Emmenthal cheese

½ cup shredded Gruyere cheese

½ cup shredded

Mozzarella cheese

freshly ground black pepper

scant 1 cup heavy cream

Mix together the softened butter and herbs. Chill.

Place the rice, stock, soy sauce, mushrooms, and parsley in a large skillet and cook for 20 minutes. Heat the oven to 375°F. Mix the cheeses together with the rice, spoon into an ovenproof dish and pour seasoned cream over. Edge with bread and top with butter. Bake for 30 minutes.

ROASTED GARLIC SALSA

Serves 4

Do not be put off by the quantity of garlic used in this salsa—the slow-roasting mellows the pungency of the cloves, producing melt-in-the-mouth sweetness. Perfect accompaniment for a tomato salad appetizer.

INGREDIENTS

4 garlic bulbs

2 rosemary sprigs

6 Tbsp olive oil

4 Tbsp water

coarse sea salt

2 Tbsp chopped fresh sage

2 Tbsp chopped fresh flat-leaf parsley

country-style bread, to serve

Preheat the oven to 325°F. Then arrange the garlic bulbs and rosemary sprigs in a roasting pan and drizzle with 4 tablespoons of the olive oil and 4 tablespoons of the water.

Sprinkle with sea salt and roast for 45 minutes, until the cloves are very soft. Cover the pan with aluminum foil if the bulbs become too brown. Discard the rosemary.

Leave the bulbs to cool for a few minutes then carefully squeeze the whole cloves out of their papery skins. Put in a bowl and toss with the herbs and remaining olive oil. Serve warm or at room temperature with toasted, country-style bread.

HERB PANCAKES WITH MUSHROOMS

Serves 6

To flavor the pancakes you can use oregano, marjoram, sage, parsley, tarragon, chive, basil, or even cilantro. If using dried herbs, reduce the quantity and soak the herbs in a little milk before blending them, drained, into the batter.

INGREDIENTS

PANCAKES

1½ cups unbleached white flour

pinch of salt

2 Tbsp chopped mixed herbs

2 eggs

1⅞ cups milk

1 Tbsp melted butter

FILLING

6 cups sliced mushrooms

milk

salt and freshly ground
black pepper

lemon juice

SAUCE

4 Tbsp butter

½ cup all-purpose flour

1¼ cups milk

½ cup shredded Cheddar cheese

1 egg yolk

grated nutmeg to taste

salt and freshly ground black pepper

Preheat the oven to 350°F. To make the herb pancakes, sift the flour, salt, and herbs into a bowl, break in the eggs and beat in the milk. Stir in the melted butter. Stand for 30 minutes. Pour a little oil into a skillet and when it is hot, spoon in a little batter. Tilt and jiggle the pan until the pancake has formed, then turn it over with a slice to start cooking the other side.

Place the mushrooms in a pan, cover with milk, season, and add a squeeze of lemon. Poach slowly until soft. Spoon the filling onto the pancakes, roll up and arrange in a large, shallow ovenproof dish.

For the sauce, melt the butter in a saucepan, stir in the flour, then the milk. As it thickens, turn down the heat, and add the cheese. Finally, stir in the egg yolk, nutmeg, and seasonings. Pour over the pancakes and bake for 20 minutes.

SESAME PIKELETS

Serves 4

Pikelets are a form of traditional pancake using a batter that is thicker than a pancake batter. This helps it to keep its shape while cooking. Make up the batter just before cooking, there is no need to let it stand.

INGREDIENTS

PIKELETS

1 cup self-raising flour

1 tsp sesame seeds

2 Tbsp butter, melted

⅔ cup milk

1 Tbsp light soy sauce

TOPPING

8 oz smoked trout fillets

2 Tbsp chopped fresh chives

1 Tbsp chopped fresh dill

⅔ cup sour cream

lemon wedges, to serve

Sieve the flour into a large mixing bowl. Add the sesame seeds and make a well in the center, gradually whisking in the butter, milk, and soy sauce.

Grease a large heavy skillet with butter. Drop 2 tablespoons of mixture into the skillet for each pikelet, cooking two at a time. Cook until the surface of the pikelet bubbles, then turn to brown the other side for 2–3 minutes. Cool on a wire rack. Repeat until all the mixture is used.

Slice the trout fillets. Mix half of the herbs into the sour cream. Spoon the sour cream onto the pikelets, top with the trout, and sprinkle on remaining herbs. Serve the fish with lemon wedges for squeezing over.

MEDITERRANEAN SALSA

Serves 4

Serve this salsa warm as part of a meal, or toss it into a pan of freshly cooked pasta.

INGREDIENTS

1 large eggplant
4 long scallions, quartered
2 plum tomatoes, quartered
1 Tbsp olive oil
salt and freshly ground black pepper

DRESSING

3 Tbsp olive oil
juice of ½ lemon
1 Tbsp chopped fresh oregano

Preheat the broiler to high. Slice the eggplant into ½-inch rounds and place on a foil-lined broiler pan with the scallions and tomatoes. Brush with olive oil and sprinkle lightly with salt.

Place the vegetables under the broiler for 8–10 minutes, turning once, until tender and lightly charred. Cut the eggplant slices into cubes and place in a large bowl with the shallots and tomatoes.

Quickly whisk together the dressing ingredients and pour over the warm vegetables. Toss well together and season to taste.

MINTED MELON MEDLEY

Serves 4

This adaptation of a Pennsylvania-Dutch recipe makes excellent use of delicious summer fruits.

INGREDIENTS

1 honeydew melon, skinned, deseeded, and cut into bite-size cubes
1 cantaloupe melon, skinned, deseeded, and cut into bite-size cubes
2 cups blackberries, blueberries, raspberries, or other in-season berries
10-oz jar mint jelly
½ cup chopped fresh mint
¼ cup granulated sugar
¼ cup water
mint sprigs for garnish

Equally divide the melon chunks and berries between four serving bowls, and stir gently to mix together. Cover and chill for at least 2 hours.

Meanwhile, melt the mint jelly in the top of a double boiler. Stir in the chopped mint, sugar, and water. Transfer the mint mixture to a small serving bowl, cover, and chill for about 1 hour.

Garnish the melon and berry salads with mint sprigs, and serve with the mint syrup.

RIGHT: MEDITERRANEAN SALSA

POTATO AND TOMATO PIE

Serves 4

A dish from the Douro region of Portugal that will become a firm favorite with vegetarians who will love its rich, slightly spicy taste. It is also the perfect way to use leftover cooked potatoes.

INGREDIENTS

6 boiled or steamed medium-sized
potatoes, thinly sliced

Red Bell Pepper Paste (see page 87)

1 bunch of parsley, stem removed and
leaves chopped

1 garlic clove, chopped

1 fresh red chile, seeded and chopped

3 Tbsp virgin olive oil, plus extra for
trickling

squeeze of lemon juice

salt and freshly ground black pepper

4 large well-flavored tomatoes, skinned,
seeded, and sliced

Preheat the oven to 400°F. Then lay out the potato slices in a well-oiled, shallow baking dish. Spread them thinly with Red Bell Pepper Paste.

Mix the parsley, garlic, and chile together with the oil. Add lemon juice and seasoning to taste and spread half over the potatoes.

Cover with the tomatoes and spoon over the remaining herb and oil mixture. Trickle over a little oil and bake for 30–40 minutes. Serve warm.

PEAS WITH CHOURICO AND EGGS

Serves 4

Topped with poached, or sometimes fried, egg, this Portuguese dish can be served for lunch or supper. If prepared without the eggs, the flavored green peas can be served with roasted or broiled chicken.

INGREDIENTS

2 Tbsp olive oil

4 oz chouriço, chopped

1 onion, finely chopped

1–2 plump garlic cloves, finely chopped

1 red bell pepper, cored, seeded, and chopped

1½ lb shelled fresh or thawed frozen peas

salt and freshly ground black pepper

4 eggs

¾ cup chopped cilantro

Heat the oil and chouriço in a saucepan for 2–3 minutes; then add the onion, garlic, and red bell pepper. Cook gently until the vegetables are tender.

Stir in the peas and seasoning, cooking for 1 minute then barely cover with water. Simmer gently until tender, 10–20 minutes depending on the age of the peas; or cook according to the directions on the pack if using frozen peas.

Meanwhile, heat some water in a wide skillet to just on simmering point. Crack in each of the eggs gently, baste the yolks with water, and poach until cooked to your liking. Once the peas are ready, drain them and mix in the cilantro.

Tip the mixture into a warm serving dish. Using a slotted spoon, remove the eggs from their water and place on top of the peas. Season the eggs and serve immediately.

BEANS WITH TOMATO SAUCE AND ONION

Serves 4

The secret of this easy to prepare dish lies in the garnish. The freshly chopped cilantro or parsley really livens up what is in essence a very simple meal.

INGREDIENTS

8 oz navy beans, soaked overnight and drained

3 Tbsp virgin olive oil

3 garlic cloves, finely chopped

3 Tbsp chopped parsley

1 Tbsp chopped mixed thyme and rosemary

1 bay leaf

pinch of dried oregano

¼–½ tsp crushed dried red pepper flakes

1 cup water

2 large tomatoes, peeled, seeded, and diced

salt and freshly ground black pepper

¼ Spanish or mild onion, very finely chopped

finely chopped cilantro or parsley, to serve

Put the beans into a saucepan and just cover with water. Boil for 10 minutes and then simmer for about 50 minutes or until the beans are tender.

Heat the oil, garlic, herbs, and crushed red pepper gently for 4 minutes. Add the water, bring to a boil, then cover and simmer for 5 minutes. Stir in the tomatoes, cover and simmer for 4 minutes.

Drain the beans and stir gently into the tomato mixture. Season and simmer for 4–5 minutes. Ladle the beans and sauce into four warmed soup plates and place a small amount of onion and cilantro or parsley in the center of each.

DEEP-FRIED MUSHROOMS

Serves 4

The use of different varieties of wild and cultivated mushrooms adds complex flavors and textures to this dish. To get really strong flavors, marinate the mushrooms for five or six hours.

INGREDIENTS

1 cup oyster mushrooms

1 cup shiitake mushrooms

1 cup open cap mushrooms, peeled and halved

⅔ cup red wine, such as burgundy

2 garlic cloves, minced

2 Tbsp red wine vinegar

2 Tbsp dark soy sauce

2 Tbsp chopped fresh chives

vegetable oil

¼ cup all-purpose flour

shredded Parmesan cheese, to serve

BATTER

1 egg

⅔ cup water

1 cup all-purpose flour

1 Tbsp shredded Parmesan cheese

Place the mushrooms in a shallow dish. Mix together the wine, garlic, red wine vinegar, soy sauce, and chives. Pour over the mushrooms, cover, and marinate for 2 hours.

To make the batter, beat the egg and water together. Sift the flour into a bowl and stir in the cheese. Make a well in the center and gradually beat in the egg mix to form a smooth batter.

Heat the oil in a wok. Then remove the halved mushrooms from the marinade and roll in the flour. Dip into the batter to coat. Deep fry them for 3 minutes, until golden. Drain and pat dry with paper towels. Sprinkle with Parmesan cheese and serve.

MEDITERRANEAN TUNA AND WHITE BEAN SALAD

Serves 4

This wonderful concoction combines the delicate flavor of cannellini beans with tuna, while at the same time providing a very nutritious meal. But do not skimp on the flavor-providers, so use only best quality extra-virgin olive oil and the very freshest basil.

INGREDIENTS

DRESSING

4 Tbsp capers

5 Tbsp red wine vinegar

1 Tbsp balsamic vinegar

2 garlic cloves, minced

¼ tsp salt

¼ tsp freshly ground
black pepper

3–4 Tbsp extra-virgin
olive oil

SALAD

2 x 6½-oz cans water-packed tuna,
drained and flaked

⅓ cup chopped red onion or scallions

4 medium tomatoes, chopped

½ cup chopped fresh basil

2 Tbsp finely chopped fresh
parsley

2 x 15-oz cans cannellini beans, rinsed
and well drained

1½ cups cooked pasta shapes or
elbow macaroni

romaine lettuce or fresh spinach leaves,
to serve

To make the dressing, combine capers, red wine vinegar, balsamic vinegar, garlic, salt, pepper, and olive oil in a jar with a tight-fitting lid. Cover, shake well, and set aside for 1–2 hours to let the flavors blend.

In a large serving bowl, combine the tuna, onion, tomatoes, basil, parsley, beans, and pasta. Just before serving, pour the dressing over the salad, and toss gently to coat. Serve on a bed of romaine lettuce or spinach leaves.

LUCKY BLACK-EYED PEA SALAD

Serves 8

Black-eyed peas are not really peas, but beans. This salad is based on a Southern dish, a region where eating black-eyed peas is considered good luck.

INGREDIENTS

2 cups large macaroni

4 cups canned, black-eyed peas, drained

1 medium red bell pepper, chopped

1 medium green bell pepper, chopped

1 medium purple onion, chopped

6 oz sliced provolone cheese, cut into strips

3 oz sliced pepperoni, cut into strips

1 2-oz jar pimento, drained

1 4½-oz jar sliced mushrooms, drained

2 Tbsp chopped fresh parsley

DRESSING

1 0.7-oz package Italian salad dressing mix, or a mixture of 2 tsp onion powder, 2 tsp garlic salt, 2 tsp ground oregano, ½ tsp ground thyme, and ½ tsp sweet, mild paprika

¼ tsp pepper

¼ cup granulated sugar

½ cup white wine vinegar

¼ cup canola oil

Cook the macaroni according to the instructions on the pack. Drain well, and transfer to a large serving bowl. Set aside.

Combine black-eyed peas, macaroni, bell peppers, onion, cheese, pepperoni, pimento, mushrooms, and parsley in a large bowl. Mix well and set aside.

Place all the dressing ingredients in a jar with a tight-fitting lid. Cover and shake to combine. Pour the dressing over the salad, mix gently, cover, and chill for 2 hours.

TRENETTE WITH TOMATO TARRAGON CREAM

Serves 4

This rich pasta dish is not for the health conscious! However, it is extremely delicious with a glass of chilled dry white wine.

INGREDIENTS

1 lb dried trenette (long, wavy strips of pasta)

dash of olive oil, plus 1 Tbsp

2 garlic cloves, minced

4 Tbsp chopped fresh tarragon

½ lb cherry tomatoes, halved

1¼ cups light cream

salt and freshly ground black pepper

freshly shredded Parmesan cheese, to serve

Bring a large saucepan of water to a boil, and add the trenette with a dash of olive oil. Cook for about 10 minutes, stirring occasionally, until tender. Drain, and return to the saucepan. Set aside, covered, to keep warm.

Heat the remaining olive oil in a large skillet, and add the garlic, tarragon, and tomatoes. Sauté for about 3 minutes, stirring occasionally, then stir in the cream. Season with salt and black pepper and cook for 2–3 minutes, until heated through. Stir into the pasta, then serve with Parmesan cheese.

PEPPER PASTA SOUFFLE

Serves 2

Perfect for a romantic dinner for two, but perfect timing is crucial! Do not remove the soufflé from the oven until your guest is seated and ready to indulge in a taste-bud treat.

INGREDIENTS

¼ lb fresh spinach fettucini

dash of olive oil, plus 2 Tbsp

1 garlic clove, minced

½ lb mixed colored bell peppers, cored, seeded, and cut into thin strips

2 Tbsp chopped fresh oregano

SOUFFLE

3 Tbsp butter, plus extra for greasing

4 level Tbsp all-purpose flour

1½ cups milk

⅓ cup freshly shredded Parmesan cheese

4 eggs, separated

Bring a large saucepan of water to a boil, and add the fettucini with a dash of olive oil. Cook for 3–5 minutes, until tender. Drain and roughly chop.

Heat the remaining oil in a skillet and add the garlic. Then stir in the bell pepper strips and oregano. Cover and cook over gentle heat until softened. Remove from the heat and set aside. Preheat the oven to 400°F.

For the soufflé, butter two small soufflé dishes. Melt the butter in a saucepan, and stir in the flour to make a paste. Gradually stir in the milk, then bring the sauce to a boil, stirring, until thickened.

Stir in the Parmesan cheese and beat in the egg yolks, one at a time. Stir in the chopped fettucini.

Whisk the egg whites in a clean, dry bowl until stiff. Fold the egg whites into the fettucini mixture, then divide between the prepared soufflé dishes. Spoon the bell pepper mixture on top of each soufflé, then bake for 20–25 minutes until risen and golden. Serve immediately.

STUFFED MUSHROOMS

Makes 16

East meets West in this recipe where the flavors of capers, Feta cheese, and soy sauce blend harmoniously.

INGREDIENTS

16 large mushrooms

¼ cup crumbled Feta cheese

¼ cup freshly crumbed Italian-style bread

½ tsp olive oil, plus extra for brushing

1 tsp light soy sauce

½ tsp ground thyme

1 tsp shredded onion

3 tsp capers, drained

Clean the mushrooms and remove the stems. Chop the stems very finely and place in a bowl. Add 3 tablespoons of the cheese and all the bread crumbs, and mix thoroughly. Stir in the olive oil and soy sauce. When well blended, stir in the thyme, onion, and capers.

Brush the mushroom caps with olive oil, inside and out. Stuff with the bread crumb mixture. Then crumble the remaining cheese over the mushrooms. Broil for 6–8 minutes, until heated thoroughly and tops begin to brown.

VEGETABLE AND CILANTRO SOUP

Serves 4–6

A light, fresh tasting soup that is ideal as an appetizer, a light lunch, or late supper dish.

INGREDIENTS

5 cups vegetable broth

1¾ cups dried pasta (any shape)

dash of olive oil

2 carrots, thinly sliced

1½ cups frozen green peas

6 Tbsp chopped fresh cilantro

salt and freshly ground black pepper

shredded cheese, to serve (optional)

Bring the vegetable broth to a boil in a large saucepan, and add the pasta with a dash of olive oil. Cook for about 5 minutes, stirring occasionally, then add the sliced carrots. Continue to cook for another 5 minutes, then add the peas and chopped cilantro. Season with salt and black pepper and simmer gently for about 10 minutes, stirring occasionally, until the pasta and carrots are tender. Serve the soup with shredded cheese, sprinkled over the top.

PASSIONATE SALSA

Serves 4

Serve this fruity salsa, chilled, with hot pancakes or creamy yogurt for breakfast or brunch.

INGREDIENTS

4 pomegranates

4 passion fruit (purple granadilla)

1-in piece stem ginger in syrup, finely
chopped, syrup reserved

2 Tbsp syrup from the jar of ginger

juice of 1 lime

1 Tbsp groundnut oil

1 tsp whole black peppercorns,
lightly crushed

1 tsp granulated brown sugar

1 Tbsp chopped fresh mint

¼ tsp coarse salt

Cut the pomegranates and passion fruit in half and scoop out the flesh and seeds into a bowl.

Mix the ginger, ginger syrup, lime juice, and groundnut oil. Spoon over the fruit. Cover and chill.

When ready to serve, sprinkle the salsa with the peppercorns, sugar, mint, and salt.

RIGHT: PASSIONATE SALSA

SCRAMBLED PASTA

Serves 4

A complete meal in a pan, this quick to prepare dish is perfect for brunch or supper.

INGREDIENTS

1 cup dried small pasta shapes

½ tsp salt

1 Tbsp vegetable oil

4 large flavored sausages (leek, pepper,
herb, or mustard)

6 slices smoked bacon, trimmed
and chopped

2 tomatoes, seeded and chopped

6 eggs, beaten

5 Tbsp milk

1 Tbsp light soy sauce

1 Tbsp butter

½ cup shredded Cheddar cheese

2 Tbsp heavy cream

freshly ground black pepper

Cook the pasta in boiling salted water for 10 minutes until *al dente*. Drain well.

Heat the oil in a large skillet and cook the sausages for 10 minutes. Remove from the skillet, slice, and return to the skillet with the bacon and tomatoes. Cook for 5 minutes. Then stir in the drained pasta.

Beat together the eggs, milk, and soy sauce. Add the butter to the skillet and pour in the egg mixture. Cook, stirring constantly for 3–4 minutes. Stir in half of the cheese and cook a further 2 minutes. Stir in the cream and spoon into a warmed serving dish. Sprinkle with remaining cheese, season, and serve.

HONEY AND ORANGE FIGS

Serves 4

Fruit is the perfect way to both cleanse the palate and whet the appetite for a hearty breakfast, a summer lunch, or a formal dinner. But make plenty—it is also a wonderful dessert served with Greek-style yogurt.

INGREDIENTS

2 Tbsp clear honey

1 Tbsp lemon juice

4 Tbsp orange juice

4 ripe figs, sliced into rings

2 oranges, peeled and sliced

4 mint sprigs for garnish

Stir the honey into the fruit juices until it has dissolved. Put the figs and oranges into a dish, pour over the honey mixture and stir together lightly. Cover and chill for at least 1 hour.

Stir gently before dividing between four chilled dishes. Garnish each serving with a sprig of mint.

FRESH FRUIT WITH PEACH GLAZE

Serves 4

**This almost-tropical salad will bring summer indoors, even in the dead of winter.
Choose fruit that is at its prime—firm and ripe.**

INGREDIENTS

1 cup fruit juice, such as peach,

pineapple-orange-guava, pineapple-

orange-banana, mandarin orange,

or raspberry

½ Tbsp lemon juice

1½ Tbsp granulated sugar

¼ tsp lemon peel

½ Tbsp cornstarch

1 cup cubed fresh pineapple

1 cup sliced bananas

¾ cup cantaloupe melon

¾ cup cubed Chinese gooseberries

¾ cup sliced nectarines

mint leaves for garnish

Combine the fruit juice, lemon juice, sugar, lemon peel, and cornstarch in a medium-size saucepan. Stir over a medium-high heat for 5 minutes, or until the mixture comes to a boil. Reduce the heat to low and cook for 2 minutes more, or until slightly thickened.

Remove the saucepan from the heat and let cool slightly; alternatively, refrigerate the glaze until thoroughly chilled.

To serve, arrange the prepared fruit in four dessert dishes. Spoon the glaze over the fruit, and garnish with mint leaves.

FISH & SEAFOOD

TASTY FISH BITES

Serves 4

Allow yourself plenty of time to make this eye-catching fish feast, as wrapping the cubed fish with strips of zucchini and carrot can be a little fiddly. Serve the threaded skewers with the sauce as part of a main meal, or thread them individually on shorter skewers as a snack.

INGREDIENTS

10 oz firm white fish, cubed

2 Tbsp light soy sauce

1 Tbsp lemon juice

2 Tbsp dry white wine

½ tsp ground ginger

1 large zucchini

1 large carrot

1 Tbsp chopped fresh dill for garnish

SAUCE

⅔ cup dry white wine

5 Tbsp fish stock

1 Tbsp light soy sauce

2 Tbsp ginger wine

1 tsp fresh ginger root, shredded

1 Tbsp cornstarch

2 Tbsp cold water

2 scallions, chopped

Place the fish in a shallow dish. Mix together the soy sauce, lemon juice, white wine, and ginger. Pour over the fish, cover, and marinate for 2 hours, turning occasionally.

Meanwhile, using a vegetable peeler, slice the zucchini and carrot lengthwise into thin strips. Blanch in boiling water for 1 minute, then plunge into cold water. Leave until cold. Soak four wooden skewers in cold water for 30 minutes.

Remove the fish from the marinade, reserving the marinade, and the vegetable strips from the water. Pat the vegetables dry with paper towels. Wrap a slice of zucchini around each fish cube and then a slice of carrot. Thread four cubes onto each wooden skewer and brush with marinade. Broil for 10 minutes, turning once, and brushing with the marinade.

To make the sauce, heat the wine, fish stock, soy sauce, ginger wine, and ginger in a pan. Bring to a boil. Blend the cornstarch with 2 tablespoons cold water and add to the pan. Return to a boil until thickened and clear. Add the scallions, and cook for 1 minute. Sprinkle the fish with dill and serve with the sauce.

BROILED JUMBO SHRIMP WITH RICE AND TOMATO SAUCE

Serves 4

INGREDIENTS

SAUCE

1 onion, chopped

1 garlic clove, chopped

1½ Tbsp oil

4 large well-flavored tomatoes, seeded and chopped

1 bouquet garni

⅔ cup medium-bodied dry white wine

12 oil-cured black olives, pitted

salt and freshly ground black pepper

SHRIMP AND RICE

1 onion, finely chopped

1⅔ cups long-grain white rice

3 Tbsp butter

1½ lb raw jumbo shrimp or large shrimp in their shells

olive oil for brushing

about 2–3 Tbsp chopped parsley

salt and freshly ground black pepper

To make the sauce, cook the onion and garlic in the oil until softened. Stir in the tomatoes and cook for a few minutes before adding the bouquet garni, wine, and olives. Simmer until thickened.

Cook the onion and rice in the butter, stirring, until golden. Add water to cover and bring to a boil. Cover the pan and simmer for about 12 minutes. Preheat the broiler. Thread the shrimp on skewers, brush with oil and broil for 7–8 minutes, turning occasionally. Drain the rice, rinse with boiling water and stir in the parsley and seasoning.

Season the sauce and discard the bouquet garni. Serve the shrimp on a bed of rice, with the sauce.

SOUTH AMERICAN MUSSEL SALAD

Serves 4

Buy mussels with tightly closed shells or shells that close firmly when tapped. Gaping shells indicate that the mussels are dead and definitely not edible. If you prefer, you can serve the mussels as you bought them, in their shells.

INGREDIENTS

5½ lb mussels in shells

salt

baking soda or all-purpose flour

¼ cup olive oil

⅛ cup sherry vinegar

½ tsp lemon juice

½ garlic clove, peeled and finely chopped

½ serrano or jalapeño chile, seeded and finely chopped

¼ tsp ground fennel

½ tsp coarse salt

½ medium red onion, peeled and thinly sliced

1 medium Florence fennel bulb, thinly sliced

¼ cup finely chopped flat-leaf parsley

½ tsp finely chopped fresh dill for garnish

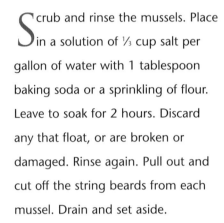

Scrub and rinse the mussels. Place in a solution of ⅓ cup salt per gallon of water with 1 tablespoon baking soda or a sprinkling of flour. Leave to soak for 2 hours. Discard any that float, or are broken or damaged. Rinse again. Pull out and cut off the string beards from each mussel. Drain and set aside.

Place the mussels in a skillet or sauté pan with a tight-fitting lid, and add 1 cup of water. Cover and steam over high heat for 5 minutes. Discard any mussels that have not opened. Transfer the mussels to a bowl and discard the liquid. When the mussels are cool enough to handle, pull off any remaining beards and remove the mussels, from their shells.

In a large bowl, mix together the olive oil, vinegar, lemon juice, garlic, chile, ground fennel, salt, onion, fennel, and parsley. Add the mussels to the bowl, toss, and transfer to a serving dish. Sprinkle with the dill and serve.

CLAMS WITH HERBS AND WINE

Serves 4

Serve this light, quick dish for lunch or supper, with baskets of fresh, crusty bread to mop up the delicious juices. To make more of a meal of it, the clams can be accompanied by a fresh green salad and sliced tomatoes.

INGREDIENTS

4 lb small clams

2 Tbsp olive oil

1–2 garlic cloves, crushed

handful of mixed parsley and cilantro
with a little oregano

1–2 well-flavored tomatoes, skinned,
seeded, and chopped

4 Tbsp medium-bodied dry white wine

salt and freshly ground black pepper

Clean, wash, and rinse the clams thoroughly. Heat the oil in a large saucepan, and add the garlic and herbs. Cook, stirring frequently, for 2 minutes. Add the clams, tomatoes, and wine. Season using plenty of pepper.

Bring to a boil, then cover and cook for 3–4 minutes until the clams open. Serve immediately.

PORTUGUESE FISH STEW

Serves 4

Calling this a stew is a misnomer, as the cooking time is quite short. To make your own fish stock, use fish bones, heads, and trimmings.

INGREDIENTS

6 Tbsp olive oil

1 fairly large onion, chopped

5 garlic cloves, minced

3 stalks celery, chopped

2 leeks, chopped

1 small bulb Florence fennel, chopped

1¼ cups well-flavored tomatoes, chopped

2 tsp tomato paste

½ red bell pepper, cored, seeded, and chopped

1 bay leaf

2-in strip orange zest

7½ cups fish stock

2¼–3 lb mixed shellfish and fish (except oily varieties), filleted

large pinch of cayenne pepper

salt and freshly ground black pepper

Cook the onion, garlic, celery, leeks, and fennel in oil for 45 minutes. Add the tomatoes, tomato paste, bell pepper, bay leaf, and orange peel. Cook briskly. Add the fish stock, boil, then lower the heat. Add the fish and simmer for 40 minutes. Add cayenne pepper and seasoning.

FRIED FISH

Serves 4

The beaten egg makes a deliciously light and crisp coating that also keeps the fish moist. Once you have tasted fish prepared in this simple way, you will wonder why you ever bothered with traditional batters.

INGREDIENTS

1½ lb hake, or any firm white fish, cut into 2-in slices

2 garlic cloves, crushed

1½ Tbsp finely chopped parsley

2 Tbsp lemon juice

all-purpose flour for coating

2 eggs, lightly beaten

salt and freshly ground black pepper

4 Tbsp olive oil

lemon wedges, to serve

Put the fish slices into a large, shallow, non-metallic dish. Mix together the garlic, parsley, and lemon juice and pour over the fish. Mix thoroughly and then leave in a cool place for 30–60 minutes.

Remove the fish from the dish, pat dry, and toss in the flour to coat evenly and lightly. Season the lightly beaten eggs and dip the fish slices in to the mixture to coat them.

Heat the oil in a large skillet, add the fish (in batches if necessary so the pan is not crowded), and fry until golden on both sides. Transfer the fish to paper towels to drain. If necessary, keep warm while frying the remaining slices. Serve hot with lemon wedges.

CRAB CAKES

Makes 4 large or 6 small crab cakes

**The serrano chiles make these crab cakes quite hot, so vary the quantity to suit your taste.
You can substitute the serrano chiles with slightly milder jalapeño peppers.**

INGREDIENTS

2 x 6-oz cans white crab meat

*2 fresh serrano chiles, seeded
and minced*

1½ Tbsp finely chopped fresh cilantro

1 cup bread crumbs

1 Tbsp finely chopped onion

1 Tbsp Dijon-style mustard

1 Tbsp mayonnaise

1½ tsp light soy sauce

¼ tsp pepper

1 tsp butter

1 tsp corn oil

*tartar or cocktail sauce, to serve
(optional)*

Empty the crab meat with juice into a large bowl. Using a fork, mix in the remaining ingredients, except the butter and corn oil, stirring thoroughly. Store in the refrigerator for a few hours or overnight, to allow flavors to blend.

To cook, form into patties—four large or six small. Sauté lightly in the butter and oil, about 5–7 minutes per side. Serve with tartar sauce or cocktail sauce.

BROILED SALMON WITH ROSEMARY

Serves 4

You can't beat the aroma and flavor of fresh rosemary, but if it isn't available use the more
flavor-packed freeze-dried rosemary in preference to dried rosemary.

INGREDIENTS

4 x 4-oz salmon steaks or 1-lb salmon

tail piece, filleted, and skinned

MARINADE

1 Tbsp cider vinegar

4 garlic cloves, minced

2 Tbsp light soy sauce

3 rosemary sprigs

6 Tbsp olive oil

1 Tbsp lime juice

salt and freshly ground

black pepper

Mix the marinade ingredients and pour over the fish in an ovenproof dish. Cover and marinate for 2 hours.

Pour off the marinade and cook under the broiler for 10–15 minutes, turning once.

TUNA AND POTATO SALAD

Serves 3–4

Canned tuna is perfectly suited to this summer lunch or supper dish. Preparation is minimal but flavor is still in abundance.

INGREDIENTS

12 oz waxy potatoes

salt and pepper

3 Tbsp olive oil

1½ Tbsp white wine vinegar

½ small onion, finely chopped

4 oz canned tuna, flaked

1 hard-cooked egg, sliced

1 small tomato, seeded and chopped

1½ Tbsp chopped parsley

sliced tomato, sliced egg, and parsley sprigs for garnish

Cook the potatoes in boiling salted water for 10 minutes. Remove from the heat and leave to cool until tender, about 15 minutes. Drain, peel, and slice thinly.

Whisk together seasoning, oil, and vinegar. Brush a little of this dressing over the bottom of a serving dish. Lay half the potato slices in the dish. Cover with half the onion, tuna, egg, tomato, and parsley. Pour over half the remaining dressing. Repeat with the remaining ingredients.

Cover and leave the potato dish for at least 1 hour. When ready to serve, garnish with tomato, egg, and parsley.

SALT COD WITH ONIONS AND POTATOES

Serves 4

There are lots of variations on this recipe, but this is the original one created by Portuguese restaurateur, Gomes de Sá.

INGREDIENTS

1 lb salt cod, well-soaked

1½ lb even-sized potatoes, unpeeled

1 Spanish onion, sliced thinly into rings

3 Tbsp olive oil

16 oil-cured olives, pitted

large bunch of parsley, stems removed
and leaves chopped

pepper

2 hard-cooked eggs, peeled
and sliced

chopped parsley and pitted black olives
for garnish

lemon wedges, to serve

Put the salt cod into a saucepan, cover with water and simmer for 15 minutes. Drain and leave until cool. Remove and discard any skin and bones. Flake the flesh.

Boil the potatoes until tender. Drain and leave them to cool, then peel and slice thinly. Cook the onion in oil until softened. Preheat the oven to 350°F.

Layer the potatoes, onion, and fish in a well-oiled baking dish, sprinkling each layer with pitted olives, parsley, and pepper. Finish with a layer of onion rings. Bake for 35–40 minutes until golden.

Arrange the sliced eggs on top of the dish and garnish with parsley and olives. Serve with lemon wedges on the side.

FISH FILLETS WITH TOMATO SAUCE

Serves 4

Fillets of whiting, sole, or flounder are suitable for this recipe. Their flavor perfectly complements the light tomato sauce.

INGREDIENTS

5 Tbsp butter

1 onion, finely chopped

1 garlic clove, minced

4 large tomatoes, skinned, seeded, and chopped

½ cup fish stock

½ cup dry white wine

1 Tbsp chopped parsley

1½ lb white fish fillets

salt and freshly ground black pepper

lemon slices for garnish

Melt 2 tablespoons of the butter in a saucepan and cook the onion and garlic until softened. Add the tomatoes, half the stock, half the wine, and the chopped parsley. Simmer, stirring occasionally, until thickened to a well-blended sauce.

Meanwhile, lay the fish fillets in a large skillet and add the remaining stock and wine, 1 tablespoon of the butter, and seasoning. Bring to simmering point, then poach gently until the flesh flakes when tested with the point of a knife.

Transfer the fish to a warmed serving plate and keep warm. Pour the juices from the skillet into the tomato sauce, add the remaining butter and boil to a sauce consistency. Season and pour around the fish.

BROILED TUNA STEAKS

Serves 4

You can serve the tuna steaks whole, or cubed and threaded onto skewers. Cube the fish before marinating, and soak wooden skewers in cold water to prevent them burning under the broiler.

INGREDIENTS

4 tuna fish steaks

1 garlic clove

small bunch parsley

juice of 1 large lemon

3 Tbsp olive oil

salt and ground black pepper

lemon wedges and parsley for garnish

Place the fish steaks in a single layer in a shallow non-metallic dish. Chop together the garlic and parsley and then mix with the lemon juice, oil, and seasoning. Pour over the fish. Leave in a cool place for about 2 hours, turning the steaks once or twice.

Preheat the broiler. Remove the fish from the marinade and broil for 3–4 minutes on each side, brushing occasionally with the marinade, until the flesh flakes easily when tested with the point of a knife. Serve with lemon wedges and parsley.

FISH WITH PARSLEY SAUCE

Serves 4

Here the ubiquitous potato is used as the base in an easy-to-make parsley sauce.

INGREDIENTS

1 small garlic clove

bunch of parsley

1 small potato, unpeeled

1 Tbsp wine vinegar

2 Tbsp olive oil

salt and ground black pepper

8 flounder fillets

4 Tbsp medium-bodied dry white wine

4 Tbsp fish stock

Chop the garlic and parsley together. Boil the potato until tender, then drain, reserving some of the cooking liquid. When the potato is cool enough to handle, peel it and mash with the garlic and parsley, vinegar oil, and seasoning, adding a little of the reserved potato water if necessary to loosen the mixture. Return to a low heat until ready to serve.

Season the fish fillets. Heat the wine and stock in a wide shallow pan and add the fish in a single layer. Poach gently for about 8 minutes, depending on the thickness of the fillets, until the flesh flakes when tested with the point of a knife. Transfer the fish to warmed serving plates and serve with the parsley sauce.

BAKED SARDINES

Serves 4

**When barbecuing is out of the question, then this is the best way to enjoy sardines.
The tomato and herb sauce keeps the fish moist during baking.**

INGREDIENTS

2¼ lb fresh sardines, scaled, gutted, and heads removed

salt and ground black pepper

1 Tbsp olive oil

2 tomatoes, skinned, seeded, and diced

1 garlic clove, finely chopped

1 small onion, finely chopped

bunch each of parsley and dill, stems removed and leaves chopped

scant 1 cup dry white wine

Preheat the oven to 350°F. Season the fish with salt and pepper and brush with half the olive oil. Use the remaining oil to grease a shallow baking dish.

Mix together the tomatoes, garlic, onion, herbs, wine, and seasoning, and spread evenly over the bottom of the greased baking dish. Put the sardines on top, pushing them into the tomato mixture. Bake for 5–6 minutes and serve immediately.

SQUID WITH BELL PEPPERS AND TOMATO

Serves 4

It is important that the squid be cooked very gently so that it is not irrevocably toughened. Serve immediately, as the flesh also seems to toughen on standing.

INGREDIENTS

2¼ lb squid, prepared

½ cup olive oil

2 onions, finely chopped

1 garlic clove, minced

2 red bell peppers, cored, seeded, and sliced

1 lb well-flavored tomatoes, chopped

1 cup fish stock

6 Tbsp dry white wine

salt and ground black pepper

2 slices firm country bread

1 Tbsp chopped parsley for garnish

Cut the squid open into two halves; then cut across into 1 inch slices.

Heat the oil in a flameproof casserole. Add the onions, garlic, and bell peppers, and cook until softened. Stir in the tomatoes and bubble until well-blended and lightly thickened. Add the stock and wine, bring to a boil and then lower the heat. Add the squid and seasoning, cover, and cook gently for 1–1½ hours, or until the squid is tender and the cooking juices have reduced to a light sauce; if necessary, remove the lid toward the end of cooking to allow the sauce to evaporate slightly.

Toast the bread, cut the slices in half and put into a warmed, deep serving dish. Pour over the squid mixture and garnish with parsley.

LUSCIOUS LOBSTER SALAD

Serves 4

Using white pepper in the court bouillon and the fruit vinaigrette maintains the pristine look of the velvety, white lobster meat in this adaptation of a classic French salad.

INGREDIENTS

2 x 1¼-lb lobsters

4–6 cups torn mixed salad greens

COURT BOUILLON

2 carrots, scrubbed and sliced

2 celery stalks, sliced

1 leek, sliced

1 sprig of fresh thyme

1 bay leaf

1 tsp salt

½ tsp white pepper

2 quarts water

2 cups dry white wine

FRUIT VINAIGRETTE

6 Tbsp walnut oil

¼ cup balsamic vinegar

½ mango or 4 fresh peaches, diced

2 shallots, diced, or 2 Tbsp chopped red onion

¼ cup diced red bell pepper

¼ cup whole cilantro leaves

salt and white pepper

Place all the court bouillon ingredients in a tall lobster pot. Bring to a boil over a high heat and continue to boil for 20 minutes. Add the lobsters to the pot and return to a boil for 12 minutes, until the shells have turned bright red. Using tongs, remove the lobsters from the pot. The bouillon can be reserved for use in a seafood stew or another dish.

When the lobsters are cool enough to handle, remove the meat from the claws and tail. To do this, twist off the claws and crack them to extract the meat. For each lobster, separate the tail from the head and body. Cut down the center of the underside of the tail, bend apart, and remove the meat. Discard the head and body. Slice the tail meat crosswise. Set aside.

Make the vinaigrette by mixing the oil, vinegar, mango or peaches, shallots or onion, bell pepper, and cilantro leaves in a small bowl. Season to taste, and set aside.

Divide the salad greens between four plates and spoon three-quarters of the vinaigrette over them. Arrange the lobster meat on top of the greens, spoon over the remaining vinaigrette, and serve.

MEAT & POULTRY

GRILLED VEAL KABOBS

Serves 4

Delicate but sometimes bland, veal responds beautifully to the strong, robust flavors of bay, parsley, and marjoram. These kabobs can be served with steamed rice and green salad.

INGREDIENTS

1¼–1½ lb veal, cut into 1–1¼ in cubes

1–2 plump garlic cloves, minced

1 bay leaf, torn in half

small handful of parsley mixed with a little marjoram, chopped

6 Tbsp medium-bodied red or dry white wine

2 Tbsp olive oil, plus extra for brushing

ground black pepper

salt

Thread the veal onto four skewers and lay in a single layer in a shallow non-metallic dish. Mix together the garlic, herbs, wine, oil, and pepper. Pour over the veal, turn the skewers, cover, and leave in a cool place for 2 hours, turning occasionally. Preheat the broiler.

Remove the kabobs from the marinade and dry on paper towels. Brush the kabobs lightly with oil and broil, turning occasionally and continue brushing with oil, until cooked to the degree required. Sprinkle with salt and serve with your favorite accompaniment.

RIGHT: GRILLED VEAL KABOBS

LAMB POT ROAST

Serves 6

Make this pot roast a special treat with the addition of red bell peppers and cilantro.

INGREDIENTS

6 Tbsp olive oil

1 large onion, chopped

3 garlic cloves, minced

1 carrot, chopped

2 red bell peppers, cored, seeded, and sliced

several sprigs of parsley and cilantro

3½ lb leg of lamb, cut into chunks

2 cups red wine

2–3 Tbsp port (optional)

salt and ground black pepper

2¼ lb waxy potatoes, parboiled and thickly sliced

2 Tbsp bacon fat

chopped parsley and cilantro for garnish

Heat the oil in a roasting pan on the hob. Stir in the vegetables (except potatoes), herbs, and meat. Pour over the wine and port, and season. Cover and simmer gently for 20 minutes. Preheat the oven to 375°F. When it is ready, put the potatoes around the meat and dot with bacon fat. Bake the dish, uncovered, for 40–50 minutes, basting until brown. Sprinkle with chopped parsley and cilantro.

PORK STEAKS MARINATED IN OLIVE OIL WITH MINT

Serves 4

Serve the pork steaks whole, or cubed and threaded onto skewers with pieces of bell pepper or whole, small mushrooms.

INGREDIENTS

4 pork steaks
ground black pepper
salt

MARINADE
1 onion, chopped
1 garlic clove, chopped
½ cup mint leaves
2 Tbsp lemon juice
⅔ cup extra-virgin olive oil

Season the pork with pepper and lay in a shallow non-metallic dish.

To make the marinade, blend the onion, garlic, mint, lemon juice, and oil to a paste and spread over the meat. Cover and leave in the refrigerator for 6–8 hours, turning the meat occasionally. Preheat the broiler.

Broil the pork for about 5–6 minutes on each side, sprinkle with salt and serve with crusty bread and a fresh green salad.

RABBIT IN RED WINE

Serves 4

The wine needed to complement this robust rabbit dish needs to be smooth, fruity, and full-bodied. Ideally, the same wine should be served with the meal.

INGREDIENTS

1 rabbit, jointed
2 onions, chopped
3 garlic cloves, minced
5 oz presunto ham or bacon, chopped
2 Tbsp olive oil
1 tsp all-purpose flour
1 cup light game, chicken, or veal stock
1 cup red wine
bouquet garni
salt and ground black pepper
chopped parsley for garnish

Cook the rabbit portions, onions, garlic, and ham or bacon in the olive oil in a heavy flameproof casserole, until the rabbit portions are brown and the onions softened. Remove the rabbit portions with a slotted spoon.

Sprinkle the flour over the onion mixture and stir it in for 1–2 minutes. Pour in the stock slowly, stirring constantly, then add the wine and bring to a boil. Simmer for 2–3 minutes before returning the rabbit portions to the casserole with the bouquet garni and seasoning. Cover tightly and cook gently until the rabbit is tender.

Discard the bouquet garni, sprinkle with parsley and serve.

PORK WITH GREEN PEAS

Serves 4–6

This dish is best made with freshly shelled green peas, but frozen peas will suffice.

INGREDIENTS

3 Tbsp olive oil
1 large onion, sliced
1¾ lb boned leg of pork, cut into large chunks
⅔ cup medium-bodied dry white wine
2 cups fresh or frozen green peas
salt and black pepper
2 large eggs
handful of finely chopped parsley

Preheat the oven to 375°F. Heat the olive oil in a heavy-based flameproof casserole, add the onion, and fry until softened. Add the meat and cook until evenly browned. Stir in the wine and allow to bubble for a few minutes. Cover the casserole tightly and cook in the oven for 30 minutes. Stir in the peas and seasoning, cover again, and cook for a further 20–25 minutes.

Stir the eggs and parsley together. Remove the casserole from the oven and stir in the eggs to thicken the sauce slightly. Serve up immediately.

CHICKEN BAKED WITH POTATOES AND GARLIC

Serves 6

An extremely easy dish to make and cook, and based on simple ingredients. It is also delicious to eat, provided that good potatoes and a fresh free-range chicken are used. Do not be put off by the amount of garlic—the flavor mellows to a mild creaminess during cooking.

INGREDIENTS

3½ lb chicken, cut into 12–16 pieces

2¼ lb yellow waxy potatoes, quartered

1 onion, sliced

20 small–medium sprigs of rosemary

salt and ground black pepper

8 Tbsp olive oil

20 unpeeled garlic cloves

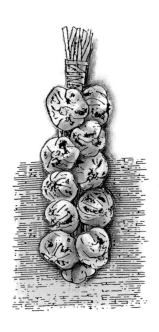

Preheat the oven to 425°F. Put the chicken pieces, potatoes, onion, rosemary, and seasoning into a large, shallow baking dish. Mix together and then pour over the olive oil. Scatter the garlic cloves over the top and bake for the dish 20 minutes.

Lower the oven temperature to 375°F and bake for a further 45 minutes or so, turning the chicken and potatoes occasionally, until the chicken is cooked through, the potatoes are tender and golden, and the garlic skins are nice and crisp on the outside.

PORTUGUESE STEAK WITH ONIONS

Serves 4

To cook the steaks to your taste, use this guide: beads of pink juice on the surface and pliant to the touch is a rare steak, abundant beads of juice and a springy touch is medium, while a well-done steak is firm to the touch.

INGREDIENTS

4 plump garlic cloves, peeled

salt and ground black pepper

2½ tsp red wine vinegar

4 beef steaks, about ¾ in thick

3 Tbsp olive oil

1 large bay leaf, torn in half

4 oz presunto ham, chopped

6 Tbsp full-bodied red wine

1 Tbsp chopped parsley for garnish

Using a mortar and pestle or the end of a rolling pin in a small bowl, mash two of the garlic cloves with a pinch of salt; then mix in the vinegar and black pepper. Rub into both sides of each steak. Leave in a cool place for 30 minutes.

Halve the remaining garlic. Heat the oil in a large heavy-based skillet, add the garlic halves and the bay leaf, and cook for 1–1½ minutes, stirring. Using a slotted spoon, discard the garlic and bay leaf. Add the steaks and brown quickly and evenly for 2–3 minutes on both sides. Transfer to warmed plates and keep warm whilst making the sauce.

Pour off most of the fat from the pan, then add the ham and cook, stirring, for 2 minutes. Stir in the wine, dislodging the sediment, and boil until slightly thickened. Season and pour over the steaks. Serve sprinkled with the parsley.

LAMB KABOBS

Serves 6–8

Variations of this recipe are found all over the Middle East, Greece, Turkey, and the Balkan States. What distinguishes each national version are the spices and the addition of some special ingredients. This recipe comes from the Lebanon.

INGREDIENTS

4 slices bread, crusts removed and cubed (about 3 cups)

1 garlic clove, minced

2 lb ground lamb

2 small onions, shredded

¼ cup ground cumin

½ teaspoon cayenne pepper

3 Tbsp finely chopped parsley

1 egg

salt and freshly ground pepper

lemon wedges, to serve

Place the bread cubes in a small bowl and add enough water to dampen them. Add the garlic and, with your hands, mash the bread and garlic with the water. Leave to stand for 10 minutes.

In a large bowl, mix together the ground lamb, shredded onion, cumin, cayenne, and parsley. Work with your hands to combine. Knead into the bread paste, the egg and seasoning to taste. Knead until everything is mixed and the meat has absorbed the liquid and become drier and smoother.

With your hands, roll the meat into 6–8 long cylinders. Pass a skewer through each cylinder and pat the meat around to secure it.

Cook the kabobs over gray-ashed coals for about 20 minutes, until brown; or under a hot broiler, turning once or twice, until done. Serve with lemon wedges.

MARINATED LIVER WITH PRESUNTO HAM

Serves 4

Prepare the liver by washing it, cutting out large tubes, and then patting dry. To avoid the meat becoming hard and tough, cut the slices a uniform thickness and do not overcook.

INGREDIENTS

1 lb lamb's liver, thinly sliced
4 garlic cloves, minced
1 bay leaf
salt and pepper
¾ cup dry white wine
1 Tbsp white wine vinegar
3 Tbsp olive oil
2 oz presunto ham, prosciutto, or bacon, chopped

Put the liver slices into a dish, add the garlic, bay leaf, and seasoning, and pour over the wine and vinegar. Cover and leave in a cool place for at least 4 hours, preferably overnight.

Remove the liver from the marinade and pat dry with paper towels. Reserve the marinade, discarding the bay leaf. Heat the oil, add the ham or bacon and cook until crisp. Add the liver and cook for about 3 minutes on each side. Transfer the liver and ham or bacon to a warmed plate, cover and keep warm.

Stir the marinade into the pan and boil rapidly until the liquid has reduced by about half. Pour over the liver and ham or bacon. Serve.

POTATOES WITH BACON AND ONION

Serves 4–6

This interesting potato dish can be served with cooked chicken, plain omelets, scrambled eggs, or can be topped with poached eggs.

INGREDIENTS

2¼ lb potatoes

1 onion, chopped

3 Tbsp olive oil

4–6 oz piece smoked bacon, chopped

¾ cup chopped cilantro or parsley

salt and pepper

Boil the potatoes until tender. Drain thoroughly and cut into slices. Meanwhile, fry the onion in the oil until softened but not colored. Remove and keep warm. Add the bacon to the pan and cook until brown and crisp. Add the potatoes and cook until browned on both sides.

Gently stir the softened onion, cilantro or parsley, and seasoning into the potato and bacon mixture. Warm through and transfer to a serving dish.

ORANGE TURKEY PAN-FRY

Serves 4

This orange sauce has an almost caramelized flavor, with the addition of maple syrup and brown sugar that bubble away to perfection with the orange juice and spices.

INGREDIENTS

1 Tbsp vegetable oil
4 turkey scallops, skinned
2 garlic cloves, minced
½ tsp ground cumin
½ tsp ground cilantro
1 leek, sliced
1 green bell pepper, cored, seeded, and cut into strips
⅔ cup orange juice
2 Tbsp light soy sauce
⅔ cup chicken stock
2 Tbsp soft brown sugar
2 Tbsp maple syrup
1 orange, peeled and segmented
1 Tbsp cornstarch
parsley sprigs for garnish

Heat the oil in a skillet and fry the turkey for 10 minutes, turning until browned. Add the garlic, spices, leek, and bell pepper and stir-fry for 3–4 minutes. Add the orange juice, soy sauce, and chicken stock and bring to a boil. Stir in the brown sugar and syrup, reduce the heat, and simmer for 20 minutes.

Add the orange segments to the other ingredients in the skillet. Blend the cornstarch with 2 tablespoons of cold water to form a smooth paste. Add to the skillet and bring to a boil, stirring until thickened and clear. Cook the turkey and orange sauce for 1 minute and serve garnished with parsley sprigs.

CHICKEN FILO PIE

Serves 6

**Packaged filo pastry is easy and convenient to use for both sweet and savory dishes.
Thawed filo can be re-frozen so there is no wastage. While working with filo pastry,
cover it with a damp cloth to prevent it drying and becoming brittle.**

INGREDIENTS

8 sheets of filo pastry, thawed

2 Tbsp butter, melted

FILLING

2 Tbsp butter

1 leek, sliced

1½ cups skinned and chopped
chicken breast meat

¼ cup all-purpose flour

¼ cup nibbed almonds, chopped

⅔ cup chicken stock

⅔ cup milk

2 Tbsp light soy sauce

2 oz sun-dried tomatoes in oil,
drained and sliced

1 stalk celery, sliced

½ cup baby corn, sliced

2 Tbsp chopped fresh rosemary

ground black pepper

Melt the butter for the filling in
a saucepan and sauté the
leek and chicken for 5 minutes. Add
the flour and cook for 1 minute. Stir
in the almonds, chicken stock, milk,
and soy sauce, and bring to a boil.
Add the tomatoes, celery, corn, and
rosemary. Season well.

Heat the oven to 400°F. Place
the chicken mixture in a deep pie
pan. Lay a sheet of filo pastry on top
of the dish and brush with melted
butter. Repeat once more. Cut the
remaining pastry into triangles.
Arrange in layers on top. Brush each
layer with melted butter. Cook in
the oven for 20–25 minutes, until
golden. Serve immediately.

LAMB CUTLETS WITH TOMATO RELISH

Serves 4

**A simple fresh tomato and herb relish, spiced up with horseradish,
is perfect with juicy, tender lamb.**

INGREDIENTS

8 lamb rib chops

2 Tbsp dark soy sauce

1 Tbsp olive oil

1 garlic clove, minced

2 Tbsp garlic wine vinegar

2 rosemary sprigs

TOMATO RELISH

4 tomatoes, seeded and chopped

1 Tbsp soft brown sugar

4 tsp red wine vinegar

2 scallions, sliced

1 Tbsp horseradish sauce

1 Tbsp dark soy sauce

1 Tbsp chopped fresh rosemary

Trim the excess fat from each lamb chop. Scrape the bone with a knife until clean. Place the lamb in a shallow dish. Mix together the soy sauce, olive oil, garlic, garlic wine vinegar, and rosemary, and pour over the lamb. Cover and marinate for 2 hours.

Meanwhile, place the relish ingredients in a pan and simmer gently for 5 minutes. Remove the lamb from the marinade and broil for 15 minutes, turning until cooked through. Reheat the prepared tomato relish until hot and serve with the broiled lamb.

MEAT PATTIES

Serves 4

Always popular with young children and teenagers, these extra tasty meat patties will become a favorite among hungry adults!

INGREDIENTS

1 lb ground beef

2 eggs

1 medium onion, chopped

1 large garlic clove, finely chopped

pinch of ground rosemary

1 blade mace, broken between your fingers

dash of soy sauce

generous helping of pepper

fine matzo meal

vegetable oil for frying

Mix together all ingredients except for the matzo meal and vegetable oil. Divide the mixture into 12 and shape into patties. Coat both sides in matzo meal.

Heat the vegetable oil in a skillet until quite hot. Cook the patties until well browned on both sides.

CHICKEN WITH APRICOTS AND OLIVES

Serves 8

An easy dish that befits an informal weekend luncheon or a formal dinner. In each mouthful there is wonderful explosion of flavors.

INGREDIENTS

3½-lb chicken, skinned, boned, and cubed

5 garlic cloves, minced

½ cup black Greek olives

¾ cup chopped ready-to-eat dried apricots

½ tsp finely shredded orange zest

5 Tbsp orange juice

2 Tbsp lemon juice or white wine vinegar

½ cup arak (anise-based Lebanese liqueur) or ouzo

2 Tbsp fresh fennel leaves

1½ Tbsp olive oil

¾ cup granulated brown sugar

Preheat the oven to 400°F. Combine all the ingredients except the sugar in a large bowl and stir carefully to mix well. Cover and chill overnight.

Transfer the chicken pieces to a baking pan and pour over the marinade, including the olives and apricots. Sprinkle over the sugar. Bake for about 30 minutes, stirring once or twice during cooking.

Remove the chicken pieces to a serving platter, and arrange the olives and apricots over and around them. Strain the cooking juices from the baking pan into a saucepan, and reduce over high heat to about half. Pour the sauce over the chicken. This dish can be served warm or cold.

LAMB WITH CRANBERRY SAUCE

Serves 4

Cranberries are traditionally associated with turkey, but are just as good with lamb. Use fresh fruit if possible, or frozen cranberries straight from the freezer. If thawed before use, they will disintegrate during cooking.

INGREDIENTS

8 x 3-oz boned lamb loin chops

2 Tbsp vegetable oil

1 cup button mushrooms, halved

1¼ cups lamb stock

2 Tbsp dark soy sauce

4 Tbsp cranberry sauce

⅔ cup cranberry juice

1 tsp tomato paste

¼ cup fresh or frozen cranberries

1 Tbsp chopped fresh cilantro

1½ Tbsp cornstarch

2 Tbsp water

Trim the lamb of excess fat. Heat the oil in a large skillet and fry the lamb for 5 minutes, turning until browned. Add the mushrooms and cook for a further 2–3 minutes. Add the stock, soy sauce, cranberry sauce, cranberry juice, and tomato paste. Simmer for 15 minutes, turning the lamb.

Stir in the cranberries and cilantro. Blend the cornstarch with 2 tablespoons cold water and stir into the skillet. Bring to a boil, stirring until thickened. Serve.

PORK WITH CLAMS

Serves 6

Despite the unlikely sounding combination of pork and clams, this is one of Portugal's most famous and popular dishes.

INGREDIENTS

2¼ lb boneless pork tenderloin, cut into
1-in pieces

2 garlic cloves, finely minced

2 Tbsp Red Bell Pepper Paste (see below)

1¼ cups medium-bodied dry white wine

1 bay leaf

2 cilantro sprigs

salt and ground black pepper

3 Tbsp bacon fat

1 large onion, finely chopped

2¼ lb clams, scrubbed and well-washed

RED BELL PEPPER PASTE

3 large red bell peppers, cored, seeded,
and quartered lengthwise

1 Tbsp sea salt

2 garlic cloves

4 Tbsp olive oil

To make red bell pepper paste, stir the bell peppers and salt; leave, uncovered, for 24 hours.

Preheat the broiler. Place the bell peppers, skin side up, on a baking sheet. Broil until the skins are charred and blistered. Peel off the skins. Purée the garlic and bell peppers in a blender or food processor, adding the oil slowly.

Mix the garlic into the red bell pepper paste and blend with the wine. Pour over the pork in a bowl, add the herbs and seasoning, and stir. Cover and chill.

Lift the pork from the marinade; reserve the marinade. Heat the bacon fat in a large flameproof casserole and cook the pork until evenly browned. Set aside the pork,

and cook the onion in the same fat until softened.

Return the pork to the casserole, and add the reserved marinade and bring to a simmering point. Cover tightly and cook gently for 1 hour. Add the clams, cover and cook for 8–10 minutes, until the clams open. Discard any that remain closed. Serve.

RICE WITH CHICKEN

Serves 4

This is a peasant-style dish using very simple ingredients. To make this dish go further, simply add more rice and boost the flavor with extra chouriço.

INGREDIENTS

1 large onion, chopped

4 Tbsp olive oil

2 garlic cloves, finely chopped

1–2 fresh red chiles, seeded, and chopped

1 red bell pepper, cored, seeded, and chopped

4 boneless half chicken breasts, skinned and cut into thin strips

1⅔ cups long grain white rice

2½ cups chicken stock

½ cup medium-bodied dry white wine, or additional stock

salt and pepper

8 oz chouriço, cut into thick slices

⅔ cup frozen green peas

10 oil cured pitted black olives, sliced

2 Tbsp chopped parsley

Cook the onion in the oil in a large flameproof casserole until softened. Add the garlic, chiles, bell pepper, and chicken, and cook gently for 2–3 minutes. Add the rice, stock, wine, and seasoning. Bring to a boil, then cover and simmer for 12 minutes.

Stir the chouriço, peas, olives, and parsley into the rice until just mixed, then cover the casserole and cook for a further 6 minutes or until the liquid has been absorbed and the rice is tender. Fluff up the mixture with a fork and serve immediately. Garnish with olives.

LENTILS AND PORK STEW

Serves 6

Prepare dried lentils (either brown or green) by placing them in a bowl and filling it with cold water. Remove and discard any that float on the surface or are discolored. Rinse under cold running water, then soak the lentils overnight.

INGREDIENTS

1 lb green (Continental) or brown lentils

2 onions, chopped

1 carrot, chopped

4 garlic cloves, halved lengthwise

1 red bell pepper, cored, seeded, and chopped

8 oz morcilla sausage or blood sausage

8 oz chouriço

8 oz fresh picnic shoulder, cut into chunks

1 bay leaf, torn almost in half

sprigs of parsley

½ tsp paprika

2 Tbsp olive oil

salt and black pepper

Put all the ingredients into a heavy-based flameproof casserole. Add sufficient water to cover by about 1 inch, bring to a boil, and then simmer gently for 30–40 minutes until the meats and lentils are tender and there is very little surplus liquid. Top up with boiling water as necessary.

Slice the morcilla sausage and chouriço, and return to the stew. Stir together and serve.

MUSCAT AND ALMOND CHICKEN

Serves 6

The muscat grape is a sweet white-green grape that gives a pungent flavor and aroma to this recipe. The almonds are used as a thickening agent.

INGREDIENTS

4½-lb free-range chicken

salt and freshly ground black pepper

½ tsp cinnamon

large pinch nutmeg

2–3 sprigs fresh lemon thyme

2–3 sprigs fresh marjoram

3 cups muscat grapes, peeled, seeded, and halved

1 cup sweet muscat wine

1 Tbsp butter

3 Tbsp slivered, blanched almonds

½ cup ground almonds

½ cup light cream

2 egg yolks

Preheat the oven to 400°F. Wash and pat dry the chicken, rub it all over with salt and pepper to taste, cinnamon, and nutmeg. Put the herb sprigs and half the grapes inside the chicken, and place it in a casserole. Pour over the sweet muscat wine. Cover and cook the chicken for 1½ hours.

Remove the chicken from the oven and transfer it to a warm serving platter reserving the juices for the sauce. Remove the herbs and grapes from the cavity, joint the chicken and cover with aluminum foil to keep it warm. Discard the herbs and grapes.

In a small saucepan, melt the butter and sauté the slivered almonds for a few minutes until just colored. Remove with a slotted spoon and set aside. Skim the fat from the chicken cooking juices in the casserole and strain them into the saucepan. Heat the juices gently until very hot, but not boiling, and stir in the remaining grapes and the ground almonds. Allow to cook for a few minutes to combine.

In a small bowl lightly beat the cream and egg yolks together. Take a spoonful of the hot chicken stock and stir it into the egg mixture. Remove the saucepan from the heat and stir in the egg mixture; the sauce should thicken.

Pour some of the sauce over the jointed chicken and sprinkle it with the sautéed almonds. Pour the remainder into a sauceboat.

SALADS

RUSSIAN DILLED POTATO SALAD

Serves 4

To reduce the calories and lower the cholesterol in this hearty dish, without diminishing the flavor, use non-fat or low-fat sour cream and yogurt. Chervil adds a subtle anise flavor, but it can be omitted if you do not like its unique taste.

INGREDIENTS

2 Tbsp white wine vinegar
2 Tbsp cider vinegar
1 Tbsp granulated brown sugar
1 tsp salt
1 tsp dry chervil (optional)
1 tsp wholegrain mustard
2 cups peeled, seeded, and diced cucumber
1 cup unsweetened yogurt
1 cup sour cream
1 Tbsp fresh lemon or lime juice
1 Tbsp dried dill
8 medium new, red potatoes
salt
mild sweet paprika

In a large non-metallic bowl, mix together the vinegars, brown sugar, salt, chervil, mustard, cucumber, yogurt, sour cream, lemon juice, and dill. Cover and chill in the refrigerator.

Wash the potatoes well, gently scrubbing so the skin remains intact. Place the potatoes in a large saucepan, cover with water, and bring to a boil. Cook over a medium-high heat for 10–15 minutes, or until tender. Cool under cold running water and drain well. Cut each potato into bite-size pieces. Fold the potatoes into the chilled yogurt and sour cream mixture with a wooden or plastic spoon. Refrigerate for at least 6 hours to let the flavors blend. Season with salt and paprika to taste before serving.

EGG AND PASTA SALAD

Serves 4

A wonderful dish for a family on the go. It is nutritious and full of valuable carbohydrates. Substitute homemade mayonnaise with a good quality bottled mayonnaise for speedy preparation.

INGREDIENTS

1 cup green or whole wheat
pasta shapes

salt

2 tsp olive oil

1 cup green beans, trimmed and
chopped

2 stalks celery, chopped

1 dessert apple, peeled, cored, and diced

½ cup walnuts

sliced chicken meat for garnish
(optional)

homemade mayonnaise or 1½–2 cups
bottled mayonnaise

freshly ground black pepper

4 eggs, hard-cooked, peeled,
and quartered

1–2 Tbsp dill

HOMEMADE MAYONNAISE

2 egg yolks

1 tsp Dijon-style mustard

2 Tbsp white wine vinegar or
lemon juice

1¼ cups olive oil or equal amounts of
olive oil and sunflower oil

salt and freshly ground white
or black pepper

Cook the pasta in plenty of boiling salted water, to which you have added 2 teaspoons of oil, until *al dente*. Drain and allow to cool. Simmer the green beans in salted water until cooked but not soft. Drain and allow to cool.

To make the mayonnaise, put the egg yolks into a bowl and stir in half of the vinegar or lemon juice, and all of the mustard. Add the oil, drop by drop, whisking constantly. After about half of the oil has been incorporated the rest can be added slightly more quickly. Continue whisking, until all the oil has been emulsified and the sauce is thick and shiny.

Beat in the remaining vinegar or lemon juice and season to taste.

Toss the ingredients except the eggs, chicken, and dill together in the mayonnaise. Season and garnish with eggs, chicken, and dill.

FAVA BEANS WITH CILANTRO

Serves 4

A liberal amount of fresh cilantro and some flavorsome tomatoes stirred into the beans just before serving, makes this a particularly interesting and memorable way of serving fava beans.

INGREDIENTS

2 oz piece of bacon, cut into strips

1 onion, finely chopped

1 lb shelled fresh or thawed frozen fava beans

salt and black pepper

2 tomatoes, peeled, seeded, and chopped

¾ cup chopped cilantro

Cook the bacon in a heavy saucepan until the fat runs. Stir in the onion and cook until softened and clear. Add the beans, barely cover with water, and simmer for 6–15 minutes (depending on the age of the beans) until they are tender, or cook according to the directions on the package if using frozen beans. Strain the bean mixture and return it to the pan. Stir in the seasoning and the chopped tomatoes, cover and heat gently, shaking the pan occasionally, for a few minutes to warm the tomatoes. Stir in the chopped cilantro at the end and serve the beans immediately.

GRILLED TOMATO SALAD WITH RED BELL PEPPERS

Serves 4

The tomatoes and bell peppers can be charred over a barbecue, as is often done in the Algarve region of Portugal, from where this recipe originates. Two or three unpeeled garlic cloves can also be broiled, then either minced and used in the dressing, or sliced and mixed with the tomatoes and bell peppers.

INGREDIENTS

1¼ lb firm well-flavored ripe tomatoes

2 red bell peppers

6 Tbsp olive oil

1½ Tbsp mild red wine vinegar

1 garlic clove, minced

salt and black pepper

round country loaves for serving

chopped cilantro or parsley for garnish

Preheat the barbecue or broiler. Grill the tomatoes and bell peppers, turning frequently, until evenly charred and blistered. Leave until cool enough to handle and then peel them.

Slice the tomatoes. Cut the bell peppers in half and discard the cores and seeds; then slice the flesh. Mix together the tomatoes and bell peppers. Whisk together the oil, vinegar, garlic, and seasoning, and pour over the vegetables. Leave for about 1 hour. Serve in hollowed out country loaves and sprinkle with cilantro or parsley.

CHINESE CILANTRO SALAD

Serves 4

This variation on a classic salad is made extra special by the cheese dressing. Keep the salad chilled until the last moment before pouring over the dressing and serving.

INGREDIENTS

8 oz head Chinese leaves or bok choy
1 ripe avocado, pitted
1 yellow bell pepper, diced
½ bunch cilantro, chopped
6 scallions, chopped
2 tomatoes, seeded and diced
4 slices bacon, broiled and chopped
1 tsp sesame seeds

DRESSING

¼ cup shredded Parmesan cheese
1 Tbsp sesame oil
4 Tbsp salad oil
1 garlic clove, minced
1 Tbsp clear honey
2 Tbsp garlic wine vinegar
¼ tsp Chinese five spice powder
2 tsp light soy sauce

Wash the Chinese leaves well and cut into bite-size pieces. Skin the avocado and cut into chunks, and add to the leaves with the bell pepper, cilantro, scallions, tomatoes, bacon, and sesame seeds.

Mix together the dressing ingredients and pour over the salad. Toss and serve immediately.

SLICED CUCUMBER SALAD

Serves 6

This refreshing salad can be served with meat, poultry, fish, or vegetables. It is crucial to serve this salad well chilled.

INGREDIENTS

2 large cucumbers, peeled, halved lengthwise, seeded, and thinly sliced
salt and freshly ground black pepper
4 Tbsp finely chopped flat-leaf parsley
1 tsp orange blossom water or shredded peel of ½ orange
½ cup olive oil
½ cup red wine vinegar
5 Tbsp superfine sugar
8 Tbsp finely chopped fresh mint

Place the cucumber slices in a strainer and toss liberally with salt. Leave to drain for 30 minutes. In a large bowl put the parsley and orange water or peel. Whisk in the oil, vinegar, and sugar until combined, and until the sugar has dissolved. Mix in the mint.

Remove the cucumber slices from the strainer and dry them with paper towels, then add to the vinaigrette. Toss gently to combine. Chill for several hours or overnight before serving.

RIGHT: CHINESE CILANTRO SALAD

LAMB AND ORANGE SALAD

Serves 4

Hot salads are sensational—the mixture of warm and cold ingredients is a treat. In this recipe, tender dice of lamb are sautéed to perfection in soy sauce and served with fennel and orange.

INGREDIENTS

1 lb lamb leg steak
1 Tbsp vegetable oil
1 Tbsp dark soy sauce
1 Florence fennel bulb, sliced
2 oranges, peeled and segmented
½ cup pecan halves
4 oz mixed salad leaves, shredded
½ cup cucumber, sliced and quartered
shredded rind of 1 orange

DRESSING

3 Tbsp olive oil
3 Tbsp fresh orange juice
½ tsp bottled horseradish
salt and ground black pepper
2 tsp clear honey
1 tsp fresh rosemary

Dice the lamb. Heat the oil and soy sauce in a skillet. Cook the lamb for 10 minutes, until cooked through. Set aside.

Place the remaining ingredients in a serving bowl. Add the lamb to the salad using a slotted spoon.

Mix the dressing ingredients. Add the cooking liquor from the skillet, stir and pour over the salad.

THREE COLORED MEXICAN SALAD

Serves 4

**This salad, influenced by Mexican cuisine, gets its name from the red, green, and yellow bell
peppers that are used. The snapper is cured by the acidic lime and lemon juices.
If you are worried about uncooked seafood, poach or steam the snapper first,
then chill the fish, and proceed with the recipe.**

INGREDIENTS

1½ lb red snapper fillets, skin removed

¼ tsp pickling salt

½ tsp freshly ground black pepper

*1 large red bell pepper, cut into very
thin rings*

*1 large green bell pepper, cut into very
thin rings*

*1 large yellow bell pepper, cut into very
thin rings*

1 red onion, very thinly sliced

1 cup fresh lemon juice

½ cup fresh lime juice

3 Tbsp tequila

unsalted (sweet) butter

kosher salt

*2 Tbsp chopped fresh cilantro
for garnish*

Arrange the snapper fillets in a
single layer in a large glass
dish. Season with the pickling salt
and pepper. Cover with the bell
peppers and onion. Pour the lemon
juice, lime juice, and tequila over it,
and cover with plastic wrap.
Marinate in the refrigerator, turning
occasionally, for about 36 hours,
until the fish is almost opaque.

Rub a small amount of butter
around the rims of four glass serving
plates. Roll the rims in kosher salt, as
you would a margarita glass. Place
the plates in the refrigerator for
about 5 minutes, until the salted
rims harden.

Drain the snapper and cut it
into 1-inch cubes. Arrange one-
quarter of the bell pepper and onion
rings on each plate, then mound
one-quarter of the fish into the
center of each plate. Garnish with
cilantro and serve.

LUXURIOUS CRAB LOUIS

Serves 4

Food writer, historian, and biographer Evan Jones has traced this salad to Solari's, a San Francisco restaurant that first served it in about 1914. This dish lives up to its name—the combination of sweet crab meat, tender artichoke hearts, and rich cream make it definitely luxurious, even indulgent.

INGREDIENTS

½ head iceberg lettuce, shredded, or

¾ cup shredded mixed lettuces

2 cups flaked fresh crabmeat

¾–1 cup homemade mayonnaise
(see page 95) or bottled mayonnaise

⅓ cup whipped cream

2 tsp Worcestershire sauce

1 tsp chopped fresh dill

2–3 Tbsp chili sauce

2–3 Tbsp grated onion

¼ cup chopped green bell pepper

1–3 Tbsp chopped fresh parsley

cayenne pepper

3–4 hard-cooked eggs, peeled
and quartered

3–4 tomatoes, cut into wedges

6–8 small bottled artichoke hearts, or
frozen artichoke hearts, thawed

Divide the lettuce between four plates. Place one-quarter of the crabmeat on top of the lettuce on each plate. In a small bowl, mix the mayonnaise with the cream, Worcestershire sauce, dill, chili sauce, onion, bell pepper, and parsley, and add cayenne pepper to taste. Spread one-quarter liberally over the crabmeat on each plate and top with eggs, tomato wedges, and artichoke hearts.

FRIED GARLIC AND GARBANZO SALSA

Serves 4–6

Serve this salsa with a selection of salads as part of a meal, or toss with a little Greek-style yogurt and eat with pita bread for a delicious light lunch.

INGREDIENTS

2 Tbsp vegetable oil

2 garlic cloves, thinly sliced

1 tsp cumin seeds

10 oz canned garbanzo beans, drained and rinsed

2 Tbsp chopped fresh mint

2 Tbsp chopped fresh cilantro

juice of 1 lime

salt and freshly ground black pepper

Greek-style yogurt for garnish

Heat the oil in a small skillet and gently cook the garlic cloves and cumin seeds for 5 minutes or so, stirring occasionally, until the garlic is softened but not colored.

Place the garbanzo beans in a serving dish, stir in the fried garlic mixture, mint, cilantro, and lime juice. Season to taste and serve while still warm, garnished with Greek-style yogurt.

MONTE CRISTO SALAD

Serves 4

**This dish is named for the sandwich of ham, turkey, and cheese served on French toast.
Serve this salad with warm crostini, if desired, to follow through on the theme.**

INGREDIENTS

1 Tbsp white wine vinegar

2 tsp Dijon-style mustard

¼ tsp dried red pepper flakes

⅛ tsp freshly ground black pepper

3 oz cooked lean ham, cut into
thin strips

3 oz cooked turkey or chicken breast,

cut into thin strips

1½ oz Jarlsberg or Munster cheese,
cut into thin strips

1 cup chopped celery

½ cup shredded carrot

½ cup thinly sliced red onion

2 Tbsp chopped parsley

In a large bowl, whisk together the vinegar, mustard, pepper flakes, and black pepper. Add the ham, turkey or chicken, cheese, celery, carrot, onion, and parsley. Toss well to coat. Cover and refrigerate until thoroughly chilled. Stir well before serving.

SPINACH NOODLE SALAD

Serves 4

Young spinach leaves should be used for this recipe. The small leaves taste and look terrific with spicy vegetables and noodles.

INGREDIENTS

8 oz flat rice noodles

2 Tbsp groundnut oil

8 scallions, sliced

2 garlic cloves, minced

½ tsp star anise, ground

2 tsp chopped fresh ginger root

2 Tbsp dark soy sauce

3 oz young spinach leaves, washed

1 Tbsp sesame oil

2 Tbsp chopped fresh cilantro
for garnish

Cook the noodles in boiling water for 4–5 minutes. Drain and cool in cold water. Heat the oil in a wok and cook half of the scallions, and all the garlic, star anise, ginger, and soy sauce for 2 minutes. Cool completely.

Arrange the spinach in a serving bowl. Drain the noodles and toss into the vegetables. Sprinkle over the sesame oil and place on top of the spinach. Sprinkle with remaining scallions and serve garnished with chopped fresh cilantro.

NICOISE SALAD

Serves 4–6

**The perfect summer salad that turns a meal into a feast. In this salad,
there is something for everyone.**

INGREDIENTS

1 head Boston lettuce

¾ cup French vinaigrette dressing

2 cups cooked French-cut green beans

2 cups diced cooked potatoes

1 cup drained and flaked canned tuna

2–3 tomatoes, peeled and quartered

*2 hard-cooked eggs, peeled
and quartered*

6 canned anchovies, halved lengthwise

*1 Tbsp chopped fresh tarragon, chervil,
or parsley for garnish*

Wash and dry the lettuce, tear into small pieces, and put in a large salad bowl. Sprinkle a few tablespoons of the French dressing over the top. Arrange the beans, potatoes, and tuna on top of the salad greens, and place the tomatoes around the edge of the bowl. Top with the eggs and anchovies. Pour over the remaining French dressing. For a final touch, sprinkle with fresh tarragon, chervil, or parsley. Serve the salad as soon as possible.

BEET AND YOGURT SALAD

Serves 4–6

**The combination of a dairy product and beets has echoes of Russian and Polish cuisines,
although these countries would use sour cream rather than yogurt. The addition of ricotta
gives this dish a distinct flavor and rich texture.**

INGREDIENTS

2 Tbsp olive oil

2 Tbsp lemon juice

1 cup unsweetened Greek-style yogurt

½ tsp cumin seeds

¼ cup ricotta cheese (optional)

salt and freshly ground pepper

1 lb cooked beets, thinly sliced

chopped mint leaves for garnish

In a large bowl, whisk together the oil and lemon juice with a fork. Stir in the yogurt and cumin seeds. With the back of the fork, mash in the ricotta, if used. Season the mixture and fold in the beets.

Transfer to a serving bowl and garnish with chopped mint leaves.

GREEK SALAD

Serves 4

This very popular and simple salad is created by combining crisp cucumber and cherry tomatoes with soft, Feta cheese.

INGREDIENTS

2 tsp red wine vinegar

½ tsp granulated white sugar

2 Tbsp olive oil

salt and freshly ground black pepper

1 cucumber

3 cups quartered cherry tomatoes

1 cup crumbled Feta cheese

½ cup finely chopped fresh basil

In a large bowl, whisk together the vinegar, sugar, olive oil, and salt and pepper to taste.

Peel the cucumber, halve it lengthwise, and remove the seeds.

Cut crosswise into ¼-inch slices. Add to the bowl with the cherry tomatoes, cheese, and basil. Toss the salad well to combine all the ingredients, and serve.

MINTED PEPPER SALAD

Serves 4

Make this cool, light, and colorful salad for a summer lunch, or picnic, but do not drizzle over the olive oil until ready to serve.

INGREDIENTS

3¼ cups dried macaroni

dash of olive oil, plus extra
for drizzling

1 yellow bell pepper, cored, seeded, and
cut into ½-in diamonds

1 green bell pepper, cored, seeded, and
cut into ½-in diamonds

14-oz can artichoke hearts, drained
and quartered

6-in piece of cucumber, sliced

handful of mint leaves

salt and freshly ground black pepper

1⅓ cups freshly shredded
Parmesan cheese

Bring a saucepan of water to a boil, and add the macaroni with a dash of olive oil. Cook for 10 minutes, until tender. Drain, rinse, then place in a mixing bowl.

Mix the remaining ingredients into the pasta. Drizzle some olive oil over the salad, then serve.

RIGHT: MINTED PEPPER SALAD

GARBANZO BEAN SALAD

Serves 6

A nutritious light meal on its own if accompanied by a green salad, or perfect as a side dish for lamb kabobs or barbecued meats.

INGREDIENTS

6 Tbsp olive oil

1 garlic clove, crushed

1 large Spanish onion, thinly sliced

1 red bell pepper, cored, seeded
and chopped

1 Tbsp dried thyme

½ tsp cumin seeds

3 Tbsp lemon juice

5 cups garbanzo beans, drained
and rinsed

salt and freshly ground
black pepper

2 hard-cooked eggs, peeled
and chopped

flat-leaf parsley for garnish

Heat the oil in a saucepan and sauté the garlic and onion over medium heat, until softened and lightly colored. After about 1–2 minutes add the bell pepper,

thyme, and cumin seeds. Take off the heat and scrape the contents of the pan, including the oil, into a large bowl. Whisk in the lemon juice to complete the dressing.

Stir the garbanzo beans into the dressing, season to taste, and gently fold in the chopped egg. Turn the mixture into a serving bowl and garnish with the parsley.

ITALIAN SALAD ON CROSTINI

Serves 4

**This flavorful salad, spread on toasted bread, makes a nice change from green salads served in a bowl.
The salad-topped crostini can also be served as an appetizer.**

INGREDIENTS

*1 large crostini or whole wheat
baguette, cut on the diagonal into
12 slices*

2 garlic cloves, peeled and halved

1 Tbsp olive oil or vegetable oil

*1 yellow bell pepper, cored, seeded, and
cut into 1-in cubes*

*2 green bell peppers, cored, seeded, and
cut into 1-in strips*

*1 long fresh red chile, seeded and
finely chopped*

½ medium onion, thinly sliced

*2 medium tomatoes, seeded and cut
into 1-in cubes*

1 cup chopped fresh basil leaves

1 Tbsp chopped fresh oregano

2 Tbsp balsamic or red wine vinegar

¾ tsp salt

½ tsp freshly ground black pepper

fresh basil leaves for garnish

Preheat the broiler. Arrange the bread slices on a broiler pan. Rub garlic cloves on the bread. Broil the bread, for 2 minutes on each side or until browned. Place three crostini on each plate.

Heat the oil in a nonstick medium-size skillet over medium heat. Add the bell peppers, chile, and onion. Cook, covered, for 15 minutes, stirring occasionally. Remove from heat. Stir in the tomatoes, chopped basil, oregano, vinegar, and seasoning. Spoon over the crostini, garnish with basil leaves, and serve immediately.

TOMATO AND CHEESE SALAD

Serves 4

The slight tang of a semi-hard sheep's cheese makes an interesting contrast to the cool, sweet, and juicy tomatoes. The chopped cilantro complements both flavors to make one of the best tomato-based salads around.

INGREDIENTS

1¼ lb well-flavored tomatoes, sliced

4 oz sheep's cheese (Manchego or Cabrales), coarsely chopped or sliced

chopped cilantro

olive oil, 4 lemon halves, and salt and pepper, to serve

Arrange the tomato slices in a shallow bowl and scatter the cheese on top. Sprinkle with cilantro. Serve with oil, lemon halves, and seasoning for each person to add, in that order.

GRAINS, BEANS, & PASTA

GARBANZO BEAN STEW

Serves 4–6

The versatile and nutritious garbanzo bean, while having a distinctly nutty flavor of its own, is also able to absorb the flavors of other ingredients. No wonder it is often added to casseroles and stews to "stretch" the meal and to make them more filling.

INGREDIENTS

1 cup garbanzo beans, soaked overnight and drained

2 Tbsp olive oil

4 oz piece of presunto ham or smoked bacon, cut into strips

1 lb pork shoulder, cubed

5 oz chouriço, thickly sliced

1 large onion, chopped

2 plump garlic cloves, chopped

1 carrot, chopped

1 stalk celery, chopped

1 leek, chopped

1 bouquet garni

1 cup vegetable, veal, or brown veal stock

salt and pepper

handful of chopped parsley

Put the soaked and drained garbanzo beans into a saucepan and just cover with water. Bring to a boil, then cover and simmer while preparing the remaining ingredients for the stew.

Heat the oil in another saucepan, add the presunto or bacon, and pork and chouriço, and brown evenly. Remove using a slotted spoon. Stir the onion, garlic, carrot, celery, and leek into the saucepan and fry until softened and lightly browned.

Stir some of the water from the garbanzo beans into the onion mixture to dislodge the sediment on the bottom of the pan. Then add the remaining water and the beans. Return the meats to the pan and add the bouquet garni and stock.

Simmer gently, partly covered, for about 1¼ hours until the garbanzo beans and pork are tender. There should only be a little water left in the pan at the end of cooking; if necessary, leave the pan uncovered so that the excess water will evaporate, or add more water if the pan becomes dry. Discard the bouquet garni, season and stir in the parsley before serving.

FETTUCINI WITH LENTIL SAUCE

Serves 4

If it is a quick but substantial meal you are looking for, then look no further. The rosemary can be replaced by fresh cilantro, parsley, or oregano.

INGREDIENTS

¾ lb dried fettucini

dash of olive oil

2 Tbsp butter

SAUCE

2 Tbsp olive oil

2 garlic cloves, minced

1 large onion, very finely chopped

1 generous cup red lentils,
washed and drained

3 Tbsp tomato paste

salt and freshly ground
black pepper

2½ cups boiling water

sprigs of fresh rosemary
for garnish

freshly shredded Parmesan cheese,
to serve

Bring a large saucepan of water to a boil, and add the fettucini with a dash of olive oil. Cook for about 10 minutes, stirring occasionally, until tender. Drain, and return to the saucepan. Add the butter and stir. Cover, set aside, and keep warm.

To make the lentil sauce, heat the olive oil in a large saucepan and sauté the garlic and onion for about 5 minutes, stirring occasionally, until softened. Add the lentils, tomato paste, and seasoning, and stir in the boiling water. Bring to a boil, then simmer for about 20 minutes,

stirring occasionally, until the lentils have softened.

Reheat the fettucini gently for 2–3 minutes, if necessary, then serve with the lentil sauce. Scatter a few sprigs of fresh rosemary over the top, and serve with freshly shredded Parmesan cheese.

SPICY GREEN RICE

Serves 4

There is something very pleasing to both the eye and the palate about a mixture of green vegetables. Packed as it is with such nutritious foods, one can overlook the heavy cream.

INGREDIENTS

2 Tbsp olive oil	1 tsp garam masala
½ cup gumbo	½ tsp ground cinnamon
1 zucchini, cut into thin strips	½ cup nibbed almonds
2 stalks celery, sliced	generous ½ cup wild rice
½ cup green beans, trimmed	generous ½ cup whole wheat rice
1 green bell pepper, cut into strips	2 Tbsp light soy sauce
1 green chile, sliced	2½ cups vegetable stock
1 tsp chili powder	5 Tbsp heavy cream
1 tsp ground coriander	2 Tbsp chopped fresh parsley
	ground black pepper

Heat the olive oil in a skillet and sauté the vegetables for 5 minutes. Add the spices, almonds, and rices, and cook for 1 minute. Stir in the soy sauce and stock, and bring to a boil. Reduce the heat and simmer for 30 minutes until the liquid has been absorbed and the rice is cooked. Stir in the cream and half of the parsley, and season. Sprinkle with chopped parsley.

PASTA GRATIN

Serves 4

Brightly colored peppers always look spectacular and, when combined with sun-dried tomatoes, garlic, and olive oil, create a truly Mediterranean dish.

INGREDIENTS

12 oz dried pasta bows	1 green bell pepper, cut into thin strips	2 Tbsp chopped fresh thyme or parsley
1 tsp salt	3 oz sun-dried tomatoes in oil, drained and cut into strips	1 egg, beaten
1 Tbsp olive oil	2 Tbsp light soy sauce	ground black pepper
2 garlic cloves, minced	⅔ cup heavy cream	¼ cup shredded Mozzarella cheese
1 red bell pepper, cut into thin strips	1 Tbsp lemon juice	

Cook the pasta in boiling salted water for 8–10 minutes. Drain. Heat the oil in a skillet and fry the garlic, peppers, and tomatoes.

Mix the soy sauce, cream, lemon juice, thyme or parsley, and egg. Season. Place the pasta and pepper in a dish. Pour on the cream mix.

Sprinkle with cheese, and cook under the broiler, until browned.

RIGHT: SPICY GREEN RICE

SALMON AND HADDOCK RICE

Serves 4

There are three varieties of rice in this simple to prepare recipe, and once you have tasted it, you will come to appreciate that each adds a distinctive flavor and texture.

INGREDIENTS

2 Tbsp vegetable oil
1 leek, sliced
1 garlic clove, minced
1 tsp dried lemon grass
1 tsp curry powder
¼ tsp turmeric
generous ⅓ cup wild rice
generous ⅓ cup arborio rice
generous ⅓ cup wholewheat rice
8 oz salmon fillet, skinned and cubed
8 oz smoked haddock fillet, skinned and cubed
2 cups fish stock
⅔ cup vermouth
2 Tbsp light soy sauce
salt and ground black pepper
2 Tbsp chopped fresh dill for garnish

Heat the oil in a large skillet and sauté the leek and garlic for 3 minutes. Add the lemon grass, curry powder, and turmeric, and cook for a further 2 minutes. Add the three different rices and cook them for 1 minute, stirring continuously.

Add the fish and pour in the fish stock, vermouth, and soy sauce. Season and bring to a boil. Reduce the heat to a simmer and cook for 30 minutes, until the rice is cooked through and the liquid has been absorbed. Sprinkle with chopped dill and serve.

CAPONATA RICE SALAD

Serves 4–6

This recipe combines caponata, a popular relish in Italian cuisine, with Italian arborio, or risotto, rice. Though arborio is preferred, it can be substituted with long grain white rice.

INGREDIENTS

1 Tbsp salt

1½ cups arborio rice

1 medium onion, cut into ¼-in dice

6 Tbsp olive oil

1 small eggplant, cut into ½-in dice

2 garlic cloves, finely chopped

3 Tbsp balsamic vinegar

3 large ripe tomatoes, seeded and cut into ½-in dice

2 Tbsp drained capers

¼ cup coarsely chopped, pitted green olives

¼ cup finely chopped mixed fresh herbs (basil, marjoram, mint, oregano, and parsley)

salt and freshly ground black pepper

Bring 10 cups of water to a boil in a large saucepan. Stir in the salt. Add the rice and cook, uncovered, over a moderate heat for about 12 minutes, until *al dente*. Drain the rice, then rinse it under cold running water, and drain again. Set aside while you make the sauce. To start the sauce, sauté the onion with 2 tablespoons of the olive oil in a large skillet over a moderately high heat. Cook for about 5 minutes, until the onion becomes soft and translucent and does not brown. Add the eggplant, garlic, and another tablespoon of the oil, and cook for about 7 minutes, until the eggplant is soft.

Transfer the cooked rice to a large bowl and toss with the remaining olive oil and the balsamic vinegar. Add the cooked eggplant mixture, diced tomatoes, capers, olives, and fresh herbs, tossing to mix well together. Season to taste, and let the salad stand for at least 20 minutes before serving.

LENTIL PASTA BURGERS

Serves 2–4

When burgers taste this good yet are so nutritious, everyone will want them. Serve them hot or cold with pita bread and salad.

INGREDIENTS

⅓ cup dried pastina (tiny pasta shapes)

dash of olive oil

7-oz can brown lentils, drained

4 Tbsp dried whole wheat bread crumbs

⅓ cup finely grated fresh
Parmesan cheese

1 small onion, chopped

1 Tbsp chopped fresh parsley

4 Tbsp crunchy peanut butter

1 Tbsp tomato paste

1 tsp yeast extract

4 Tbsp hot water

sunflower oil

Bring a large saucepan of water to a boil, and add the pastina and the olive oil. Cook for about 8 minutes, stirring occasionally, until tender. Drain the pasta, and allow to cool slightly.

Transfer the pasta to a large mixing bowl. Combine with the brown lentils, bread crumbs, Parmesan cheese, onion, and parsley. Mix well and set aside.

Place the peanut butter, tomato paste, and yeast extract in a separate bowl and stir together with the hot water. Add this to the pasta mixture, and mix well.

Using damp hands, divide the mixture into four equal portions, and form into burger shapes. Heat the oil for shallow frying, and fry the burgers for about 5 minutes on each side. Serve hot or cold.

BUCATINI WITH TOMATOES

Serves 4

**When you serve this dish, do not be surprised when your guests ask for second servings.
Though very filling, the temptation to have more is hard to resist.**

INGREDIENTS

¾ lb dried bucatini (long hollow
pasta tubes)

dash of olive oil

2 garlic cloves, minced

1 onion, finely chopped

1 lb carton puréed tomatoes

4 Tbsp chopped fresh basil

salt and freshly ground black pepper

butter

⅔ cup freshly grated Pecorino or
Parmesan cheese

Bring a large saucepan of water to a boil, and add the bucatini with the olive oil. Cook for about 10 minutes, stirring occasionally, until tender. Drain and set aside.

Preheat the oven to 400°F. Place the garlic, onion, tomatoes, fresh chopped basil, and seasoning in a large skillet, and heat until simmering. Cook for about 5 minutes, then remove the skillet from the heat.

Grease a shallow ovenproof dish with butter, and arrange the bucatini on top. Curl it around to fit the dish, until it is tightly packed with the pasta.

Spoon the tomato mixture over the top, prodding the pasta to ensure the sauce sinks to the bottom of the dish. Sprinkle with cheese, and bake for 25–30 minutes, until crisp and golden. Cut in wedges to serve.

RAVIOLI WITH CHEESE SAUCE

Serves 6

Fresh mint tastes a million times better than dried, so try to use it to give this dish the full flavor it deserves.

INGREDIENTS

PASTA DOUGH

2 cups all-purpose flour, plus extra for dusting

⅔ Tbsp salt

6 Tbsp spinach liquid strained from 1½ lb chopped spinach, cooked for 5 minutes

2 eggs

CHEESE SAUCE

2 Tbsp butter

¼ cup all-purpose flour

2½ cups warm milk

1 tsp Dijon-style mustard

1½ cups shredded mature Cheddar cheese

salt and freshly ground black pepper

RAVIOLI FILLING

2 Tbsp olive oil, plus extra

1 onion, very finely chopped

2 cups frozen green peas

3 Tbsp chopped fresh mint

1 egg, beaten and mixed with 2 tsp tomato paste, for brushing

fresh mint sprigs for garnish

To make the dough, combine the flour and salt in a mixing bowl, and make a well in the center. Break the eggs into the well and gradually add the spinach liquid. Mix until the dough forms clumps.

Turn out onto a lightly floured surface and knead for 5 minutes. Wrap the dough in plastic wrap and leave to rest at room temperature for at least 30 minutes.

To make the sauce, melt the butter in a saucepan, and stir in the flour. Cook for 30 seconds, then remove from the heat. Stir in the milk gradually. Return the pan to a medium heat, stirring until the sauce thickens and boils.

Add the mustard and cheese, and season. Continue to cook, stirring constantly, until the cheese melts. Remove from the heat until needed.

To make the filling, heat the oil in a skillet and sauté the onion, until softened. Add the frozen peas, cover and cook for 7 minutes, until cooked through. Stir in the mint, remove from the heat, and season. Allow to cool slightly before transferring to a blender or food processor, and puréeing to a slightly coarse texture. Allow to cool.

Unwrap the dough and divide in half. Roll out one half to a rectangle slightly larger than 14 inches by 10 inches. Trim to neaten. Roll out the remaining half to the same size, but do not trim.

Place half teaspoonsful of the ravioli filling, in lines spaced about ¾ inch apart, all over the trimmed dough. Brush the egg mixture around the filling to cover the dough. Lay the other rectangle of dough on top and, starting at one end, seal in the filling by lightly pressing the dough and gently flattening the filling to make little packets. Using a knife or pastry wheel, cut between the fillings to make the squares of ravioli.

To cook, bring a saucepan of water to a boil, and add the ravioli with a dash of olive oil. Cook for about 5 minutes, until tender. Drain, cover, and set aside to keep warm. Reheat the sauce and serve separately. Garnish with mint sprigs.

SAUTEED FLAGEOLET BEANS WITH FUSILLI

Serves 2–4

Though the flavor of the garlic is strong it does not dominate the delicate tarragon. Serve as a main course or as an accompaniment.

INGREDIENTS

3½ cups dried fusilli (short twists of pasta)

dash of olive oil, plus 4 Tbsp

3 garlic cloves, minced

1 large onion, sliced

2 Tbsp chopped fresh tarragon

14-oz can flageolet beans, drained

salt and freshly ground black pepper

green salad, to serve

Bring a saucepan of water to a boil. Add the fusilli and dash of oil. Cook for 10 minutes, until tender. Drain and set aside.

Heat the olive oil in a large skillet and sauté the garlic and onion until browned slightly. Add the tarragon and beans, and season to taste. Cook for 2–3 minutes, then stir in the fusilli. Cook, to heat through. Serve with salad.

PASTA WITH LEMON AND OIL

Serves 4–6

Italian cuisine meets the exotic Middle East in this light dish that melds pasta with lemon and herbs.

INGREDIENTS

1 lb dried macaroni or spaghetti

½ cup olive oil

1 cup finely chopped parsley

5 or 6 finely chopped fresh mint or basil leaves

juice of 1 lemon

salt and freshly ground black pepper

Bring a large saucepan of salted water to a boil, then add the dried macaroni or spaghetti and a drop or two of the olive oil. Bring back to a boil and simmer for about 15 minutes, or until just tender. Drain the pasta thoroughly before returning it to the pan.

Add the chopped fresh herbs and toss with the pasta. Add the remaining olive oil, lemon juice, and season the mixture to taste. Continue to toss until the pasta has absorbed most of the liquid. The dish may be served either hot or cold after chilling in the refrigerator.

CREAMY LEEK AND PASTA FLAN

Serves 6–8

**Whether served hot straight from the oven or chilled, this pasta flan tastes wonderful.
The perfect contribution to a bring-a-plate party.**

INGREDIENTS

1½ cups dried orecchiette (ear shape pasta)

dash of olive oil, plus 3 Tbsp

a little all-purpose flour

¾ lb packaged puff pastry, thawed if frozen

2 garlic cloves, minced

1 lb leeks, washed, trimmed, and cut into 1-in pieces

2 Tbsp chopped fresh thyme

2 eggs, beaten

⅔ cups light cream

salt and freshly ground black pepper

1¼ cups shredded Cheddar cheese

Bring a large saucepan of water to a boil, and add the orecchiette with a dash of olive oil. Cook for about 10 minutes, stirring occasionally, until tender. Drain and set aside.

Dredge the work surface with flour and roll out the puff pastry to line a greased, 10-inch, loose-bottomed, fluted flan dish. For best results, chill in the refrigerator for at least 10 minutes.

Preheat the oven to 375°F. Heat the remaining olive oil in a large skillet and sauté the garlic, leeks, and thyme for about 5 minutes, stirring occasionally, until they become softened and tender. Then stir in the orecchiette, and continue to cook the mixture for a further 2–3 minutes.

Place the beaten eggs in a small bowl, then whisk in the cream, salt, and pepper. Transfer the leek and pasta mixture to the pastry case, spreading it out evenly. Pour the egg mixture over the top, then sprinkle with cheese. Bake for about 30 minutes, until the mixture is firm and the pastry crisp.

HERBED MUSHROOM PASTA SALAD

Serves 4–8

Any small pasta shapes can be used in this dish. It can be served as a main course for a luncheon, or as a side dish for cold meats.

INGREDIENTS

1 lb dried pasta shapes

dash of olive oil

½ lb cup mushrooms, quartered

1 red bell pepper, cored, seeded, and cut into ½-in squares

1 yellow bell pepper, cored, seeded, and cut into ½-in squares

1 cup pitted black olives

4 Tbsp chopped fresh basil

2 Tbsp chopped fresh parsley

DRESSING

2 tsp red wine vinegar

1 tsp salt

freshly ground black pepper

4 Tbsp extra-virgin olive oil

1 garlic clove, minced

1–2 tsp Dijon-style mustard

Bring a large saucepan of water to a boil, and add the pasta and a dash of olive oil. Cook for about 10 minutes, until tender. Drain, and rinse under cold running water. Drain well again.

Place the cooked pasta in a large salad bowl, and add the remaining ingredients. Toss together to combine.

To make the dressing, place all the ingredients in a bottle with a tightly-fitting lid or a screw-top jar and shake well. Pour the dressing over the salad and toss together. Cover and refrigerate for at least 30 minutes, then toss again before serving.

TOMATO RICE

Serves 4

The character of this Portuguese dish comes from using well flavored, sweet, and juicy tomatoes. If the rice is soggy at the end of cooking, the Portuguese would say *"malandrinho,"* meaning naughty!

INGREDIENTS

2 Tbsp olive oil

1 large onion, finely chopped

1 garlic clove, finely chopped

2 ripe, well-flavored tomatoes, skinned, seeded, and finely chopped

generous 1 cup long-grain white rice

boiling water

2 Tbsp chopped parsley

salt and pepper

Heat the oil in a saucepan, add the onion and garlic, and fry until softened but not brown. Stir in the tomatoes and cook for a further 5 minutes before adding the rice. Stir to coat with the vegetables and oil; then add boiling water to 2½ times the volume of the rice. Bring to a boil, cover, and cook over a low heat until the rice is tender and all the liquid has been absorbed. Stir in the chopped parsley and seasoning to taste. Serve while it is still nice and hot.

FAVA BEANS WITH BACON AND HERBS

Serves 4

Serve for luncheon with a crisp, crunchy green salad and lots of fresh crusty bread.

INGREDIENTS

4 oz piece of bacon, cut into strips

1 onion, chopped

1 garlic clove, chopped

1 lb shelled fresh or frozen fava beans, thawed

large sprig of mint

large sprig of parsley, chopped

1 bay leaf

salt and pepper

Cook the bacon in a heavy saucepan until the fat runs. Stir in the onion and garlic, and cook gently until they are softened.

Stir in the beans, herbs, and seasoning. Barely cover with water and simmer for 6–15 minutes, until the beans are tender; or cook according to the directions on the package if using frozen beans. Strain and discard the bay leaf and mint. Serve immediately.

RIGHT: FAVA BEANS WITH BACON AND HERBS

BRAISED LENTILS

Serves 4

A large, steaming bowl of these well flavored lentils is a meal in itself.

INGREDIENTS

2 Tbsp olive oil

1 onion, finely chopped

1 plump garlic clove, minced

1 leek, chopped

1 carrot, chopped

1 potato, chopped

1 large tomato, peeled and chopped

1 generous cup brown lentils, washed, picked through, and soaked

2½ cups veal, chicken, or vegetable stock

1 bouquet garni

2 anchovy fillets, chopped

2 tsp wine vinegar

salt and pepper

Heat the oil in a saucepan, add the onion and cook until softened. Stir in the garlic, leek, carrot, and potato, and cook for 4–5 minutes. Stir in the tomato, then the lentils.

Add the stock and bouquet garni, bring to a boil and simmer for 30 minutes. Discard the bouquet garni. Purée one-third of the lentils with the anchovies and vinegar. Reheat, season, and serve.

TABBOULEH

Serves 4

A great salad to take on picnics as it travels well and does not suffer from being served unchilled. It can be prepared in advance, but must be stored in a refrigerator.

INGREDIENTS

½ cup chicken stock

½ cup water

¼ cup fresh lemon juice

¼ cup olive oil

¾ cup couscous, made of wheat

semolina (farina), or bulgur (cracked) wheat

½ seedless cucumber, cut into ¼-in pieces

2 Tbsp tomato, peeled, seeded, and finely diced

½ cup finely chopped scallions

salt

1 tsp chopped fresh basil

1 loosely packed cup chopped fresh parsley

½ loosely packed cup chopped fresh mint

mint sprigs and cucumber slices for garnish

In a saucepan, combine the stock, water, half the lemon juice, and 1 tablespoon of the oil. Bring to a boil and stir in the couscous. Cover the pan, remove from the heat, and stand for 5 minutes.

In a bowl, mix the cucumber, tomato, scallion, olive oil, lemon juice, and salt. Add the couscous and herbs, and chill.

PROVENCAL GREEN BEANS WITH PASTA

Serves 4–6

A delicious way to serve green beans—piping hot and liberally sprinkled with freshly shredded Parmesan cheese. Pecorino cheese can be substituted for the Parmesan.

INGREDIENTS

2 Tbsp olive oil

3 garlic cloves, minced

1 onion, chopped

3 Tbsp chopped fresh thyme

1 lb whole green beans, trimmed

14-oz can chopped tomatoes

2 heaped Tbsp tomato paste

scant 2 cups vegetable broth

⅔ cup dry red wine

salt and freshly ground black pepper

1 lb dried pasta (any shape)

dash of olive oil

2 Tbsp butter

freshly shredded Parmesan cheese, to serve

Heat the oil in a large skillet, and sauté the garlic and onion for about 3 minutes, until softened. Add the thyme, beans, tomatoes, tomato paste, vegetable broth, and wine, and season with salt and pepper. Stir well to combine. Cover and cook gently for 25–30 minutes, until the beans are tender. Remove the lid and cook for a further 5–8 minutes, stirring occasionally, until the sauce has thickened slightly.

While the beans are cooking, bring a large saucepan of water to a boil, and add the pasta and the dash of olive oil. Cook for about 10 minutes, stirring occasionally, until tender. Drain the pasta and return to the saucepan. Toss in butter and black pepper.

Serve the pasta in bowls with the beans and the shredded Parmesan sprinkled over the top.

SIDE DISHES & ACCOMPANIMENTS

CHEESE BALLS

Makes about 25–30 balls

In the original Lebanese recipe a special cheese called *gibna arish* would be used. Here, unripened Chèvre log blended with Feta cheese makes a very acceptable substitute.

INGREDIENTS

8-oz log unripened Chèvre cheese

6 oz Feta cheese

½ tsp ground cumin

¼ tsp cayenne pepper

3 Tbsp finely chopped mint or thyme leaves

4 Tbsp olive oil

Combine the cheeses, cumin, and cayenne in a bowl and mash together thoroughly. Take out small spoonfuls of the mixture and form into bite-sized balls. Roll the balls in the chopped herbs and chill until firm.

Before serving, arrange the cheese balls on a plate and drizzle the olive oil over them.

ARTICHOKES WITH TOMATO SAUCE

Serves 4

Globe artichokes sadly make very few appearances in home cooking because many of us suspect that they are difficult to prepare. But nothing could be further from the truth, as this recipe proves.

INGREDIENTS

4 large globe artichokes

1–2 Tbsp oil

1 large onion, chopped

2 garlic cloves, chopped

15-oz can tomatoes, mashed

1 Tbsp tomato paste

2 Tbsp chopped fresh oregano

lemon juice

salt and freshly ground black pepper

Trim and rinse the artichokes thoroughly under the cold tap and leave them upside down to drain. Bring a very large pan of salted water to a boil, add the artichokes and boil fast for 30–50 minutes, depending on their size. When an outer leaf comes away at a gentle tug, the artichokes are ready. Meanwhile, make the sauce. Heat the oil in a pan and fry the onion and garlic until transparent. Add the tomatoes, tomato paste, and oregano, and reduce until the sauce is of pouring consistency. Season and add a dash of lemon juice.

Drain the artichokes once they are ready. When cool, pull out the tiny inner leaves together with the hairy inedible choke. Spoon some tomato sauce into the center. Then stand each artichoke in a pool of sauce on an individual dish and serve immediately.

ORANGE AND WATERCRESS SALAD IN CITRUS DRESSING

Serves 4

This refreshing salad has a Caribbean flair, but the ingredients are easily available. To keep the watercress in the best condition for use, store it in a bowl of water in a refrigerator until required.

INGREDIENTS

1 large bunch watercress

2 medium oranges, peeled, seeded, segmented, and sliced crosswise

⅓ cup chopped scallions

CITRUS DRESSING

1½ Tbsp fresh lemon juice

1 Tbsp orange juice

¼ tsp crushed dried mint

2 Tbsp olive oil

¼ tsp salt

Rinse the watercress well. Remove and discard large stems, dry the leaves on paper towels, and chill. Place the watercress on a plate, and add orange segments and scallions. In a small bowl, mix together the dressing ingredients to combine. Pour the dressing over the salad and toss gently. Serve immediately.

RIGHT: ORANGE AND WATERCRESS SALAD

TURKISH CUCUMBER SALAD

Serves 4

With every mouthful of this salad, your palate is in for a treat. For while the flavors blend beautifully, sometimes it is the taste of the raisins, nuts, or mint that predominates.

INGREDIENTS

1 large cucumber, shredded

1 cup unsweetened yogurt

2 Tbsp blanched golden raisins

2 Tbsp chopped walnuts

1 small onion, finely chopped

salt and freshly ground black pepper

1 tsp chopped fresh mint

Place the cucumber, yogurt, raisins, walnuts, and onion in a large serving bowl and stir to combine. Season to taste.

Blend in half the mint. Serve in the bowl or on four individual plates, with the remaining mint sprinkled on top to garnish.

NEW POTATOES WITH CILANTRO

Serves 4

Cilantro makes a welcome change to the traditional parsley or chives.

INGREDIENTS

2¼ lb small new potatoes

4 Tbsp butter

4 scallions

1 bunch fresh cilantro,
finely chopped

salt and pepper

Boil the potatoes until just tender, drain, and keep warm. Melt the butter in a saucepan, and add the scallions. Cook the scallions until soft, and add the cilantro.

Return the potatoes to the pan and mix well with scallion mixture. Season to taste and serve.

POTATO GNOCCHI

Serves 4

This dish can be prepared in advance. Store, covered, in a refrigerator until needed.

INGREDIENTS

2 lb potatoes

2¼ cups whole wheat flour

salt

1 egg

4 Tbsp butter

4 oz Mozzarella cheese, thinly sliced

TOMATO SAUCE

1–2 Tbsp oil

1 onion, chopped

2 garlic cloves, chopped

15-oz can tomatoes, mashed

2 Tbsp tomato paste

salt and freshly ground black pepper

1 Tbsp fresh oregano, chopped

Preheat the oven to 375°F. Peel the potatoes and boil until soft, and then mash well. Add the flour, salt, egg, and half the butter. Shape into balls.

For the sauce, heat the oil, and fry the onion and garlic until soft. Add the tomatoes, tomato paste, seasoning, and herbs, and simmer for 5 minutes.

Layer the gnocchi balls in an ovenproof dish with the cheese, and dot with butter. Pour over the sauce. Finish with a cheese layer. Bake in the oven for 20 minutes.

STUFFED TOMATOES

Serves 4

**These tomatoes add color to any meal, be it a roasted or broiled meat, poultry, or fish dish.
They are also a welcome change for lacto-ovo vegetarians tired of the usual array of
steamed vegetables.**

INGREDIENTS

*4 very large, ripe, well-flavored
tomatoes, or 8 smaller ones, halved
horizontally*

2 handfuls fresh bread crumbs

2 garlic cloves, finely chopped

handful of chopped parsley

3 Tbsp olive oil

2 eggs, beaten

salt and pepper

butter for greasing

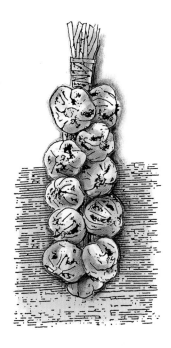

Scoop out the insides of the tomatoes carefully. Season the inside of the tomatoes, turn them upside down and leave to drain. Mix together the remaining ingredients.

Place the tomatoes the right way up in a greased baking dish and fill with the bread crumb mixture. Bake at 400°F for about 15 minutes. Serve the tomatoes hot.

STUFFED VINE LEAVES

Makes about 30 stuffed vine leaves

Stuffed vine leaves, or *dolmades,* are common to the cuisines of many Mediterranean and Middle Eastern cultures. The distinctive things about these *dolmades* are the absence of meat and the fact that they are best served cold.

INGREDIENTS

6-oz packet vine leaves (about 35)
4 Tbsp olive oil
2 Tbsp pine nuts
1 large onion, finely chopped
⅓ cup long-grain white rice
salt and pepper
½ cup boiling water
1 Tbsp raisins
1½ Tbsp finely chopped mint
½ Tbsp cinnamon
juice of 2 lemons
lemon wedges, to serve

Remove the vine leaves from the packet, separate them, place in a large bowl and pour boiling water over them. Allow to soak for 15 minutes, then drain. Return to the bowl, pour cold water on them, and soak for a further 10 minutes, then drain thoroughly on paper towels.

Heat 1 tablespoon of the olive oil in a large skillet. Add the pine nuts and sauté, stirring, for about 4 minutes, or until the pine nuts are golden. Remove the pine nuts with a slotted spoon and reserve to one side. Add another 1 tablespoon of olive oil to the pan, and stir in the onions. Sauté for about 5–6 minutes until softened, then add the rice, and season to taste. Stir the rice until it is coated with the oil, then pour in the boiling water to cover. Reduce the heat, cover, and cook over medium heat for about 5 minutes. Take off the heat and allow to sit for about 20 minutes, until the water has been absorbed and the rice is tender. Stir in the raisins, reserved pine nuts, chopped mint, and cinnamon.

Lay a vine leaf flat, and spoon 2 tablespoons of the rice mixture near the stem end. Roll the leaf one turn over the mixture, then tuck in the sides of the leaf toward the center. Continue to roll the leaf until you reach the end. Squeeze the bundle to remove excess moisture. Repeat for the remaining leaves.

If there are any vine leaves left over, lay them on the bottom of a lightly oiled casserole. Arrange the stuffed leaves in a single layer on top. Pour over the lemon juice and just enough hot water to cover. Drizzle over the remaining olive oil. Weigh the stuffed leaves down with a plate. Cover tightly and cook over high heat for about 4 minutes, then lower the heat and simmer for about 40 minutes. Remove the casserole from the heat, uncover and allow to cool in the cooking liquid. When cold, remove the stuffed leaves with a slotted spoon and arrange on a platter. Serve at room temperature or chilled, together with lemon wedges to squeeze over.

ROASTED CORN SALSA

Serves 8

**Fill a baked potato with a spoonful of sour cream and top with this fragrant salsa for a super light lunch.
Remember to choose the freshest, juiciest corn cobs.**

INGREDIENTS

4 corn on the cob

juice of 2 limes, freshly squeezed

4 tomatoes, seeded and finely diced

2 red onions, finely chopped

4 Tbsp chopped fresh cilantro

3 Tbsp olive oil

salt and freshly ground black pepper

Brush the corn cobs with a little of the lime juice and sprinkle with salt. Gently barbecue or broil for 20–30 minutes, turning them over occasionally, until tender and golden. Using a knife, slice down the cobs to remove the kernels. Place the corn kernels in a bowl with the tomatoes, red onions, and coriander. Whisk together the olive oil and remaining lime juice. Season to taste and pour over the corn kernel mixture. Toss well to mix and serve the salsa while still slightly warm, or cover and chill in the refrigerator for up to 2 hours.

SUNSHINE SALSA

Serves 4

This beautiful salsa brings a ray of sunshine to the dining table. Serve it as a refreshing accompaniment to fish.

INGREDIENTS

2 yellow tomatoes, thinly sliced

2 ripe red tomatoes, thinly sliced

2 small oranges, peeled, thinly sliced
into rounds, and seeded

1 tsp bottled pink peppercorns, lightly
crushed

1 garlic clove, finely chopped

2 Tbsp chopped fresh parsley,
cilantro or chives

2 Tbsp extra virgin olive oil

salt and freshly ground
black pepper

Arrange the tomatoes and orange slices on a large round serving platter. Whisk together the peppercorns, garlic, herbs, olive oil, and plenty of seasoning. Drizzle over the salsa and serve immediately.

EGGPLANT SALAD

Serves 4–6

If you find this dish too tart, do as the Hungarians do and add a pinch of granulated sugar.

INGREDIENTS

2 eggplants

olive oil for brushing

1 medium onion, chopped

¼ cup finely chopped fresh parsley

2 tsp salt

1 tsp black pepper

½ cup olive oil

⅔ cup vinegar

lettuce leaves, to serve

tomato wedges or cherry tomatoes, and

pitted black olives for garnish

Preheat the broiler to hot. Remove the plant stalk from the eggplants and slice the eggplants into thick rounds. Brush both sides with a little olive oil, place on a wire rack, and broil for 3–5 minutes on each side, until soft. Let cool, then peel and chop into dice. Mix the eggplant with the onion and parsley in a large bowl. Add the salt and pepper. Whisk the oil and vinegar together in a small bowl, and add to the eggplant mixture. Toss well to coat evenly. Serve the salad on a bed of lettuce leaves, and garnish with tomato wedges or cherry tomatoes, and pitted olives.

RIGHT: EGGPLANT SALAD

GARLIC MUSHROOMS

Serves 4

For a long time most restaurants offered garlic mushrooms, but for some unknown reason, they fell out of favor. Here is a reminder of how good they are.

INGREDIENTS

16 open mushrooms, about

1½ in across

2 slices whole wheat bread, crumbed

⅝ cup warm milk

4 garlic cloves

1 cup fresh mixed herbs

a little oil

salt and freshly ground black pepper

sprigs of watercress

Preheat the oven to 350°F. Wipe the mushroom caps clean, remove the stalks, chop finely, and reserve the stalks.

Soak the bread crumbs in milk until soft, then squeeze out excess milk. In a mortar, pound the garlic and herbs with enough oil to make a paste. Pound in the reserved stalks. Mix together with the bread crumbs and season well with salt and pepper.

Spoon the filling into the mushroom caps and arrange them in a lightly oiled ovenproof dish. Bake for about 15 minutes until mushrooms are soft and juicy, and the filling has crisped a little on the top. Serve piping hot with sprigs of peppery watercress.

MAMA MIA'S PASTA SALAD

Serves 4

While brimming with Italian ingredients, this pasta salad—like most pasta salads is American. Italians prefer their noodles warm, but Americans have been eating them cold since the early 1900s. This salad can be embellished with salami, pastrami, or ham.

INGREDIENTS

1 lb dried pasta shapes (rotini, penne, fusilli, or shells)

½ cup sun-dried tomatoes, soaked in hot water for 5 minutes, then drained

½ lb smoked Mozzarella, cut into ½-in cubes

1 1-lb can garbanzo beans, drained and rinsed

10–20 small strips of bottled pepperoncini

½ tsp dried red pepper flakes

1 loosely packed cup fresh, flat-leaf parsley leaves

DRESSING

2 garlic cloves

1 Tbsp Dijon-style mustard

⅓ cup red wine vinegar

2 Tbsp balsamic vinegar

1 Tbsp water

½ cup olive oil, or ½ cup of juice extracted from red bell peppers with 2 tsp of vegetable oil added

salt

Cook the pasta in a large saucepan of boiling salted water until *al dente*, then rinse under cold running water and drain well. Transfer the pasta to a very large bowl.

Make the dressing by blending all dressing ingredients in a blender or food processor until smooth. Pour the dressing over the pasta and toss to coat evenly. Stir in the sun-dried tomatoes, Mozzarella, garbanzo beans, pepperoncini, red pepper flakes, and parsley. Cover and refrigerate for 4 hours. This dish should be served thoroughly chilled.

TEX-MEX CORN AND BLACK BEAN SALAD

Serves 6–8

This healthy salad has only the smallest amount of oil in it. The liquid for the dressing being provided instead by juice from the corn. Unlike some Tex-Mex dishes, this one does not depend on fat for its flavor.

INGREDIENTS

1 x 12-oz can whole-kernel corn, drained with juice reserved

1 x 15-oz can black beans, drained and rinsed

1 red bell pepper, finely chopped

½ cup chopped scallions

½ cup chopped red onion

1 garlic clove, finely chopped

1 medium tomato, chopped

1 jalapeño chile, seeded and finely chopped (optional)

cilantro sprigs or red onion wedges for garnish

DRESSING

¼ cup corn juice, measured out from the reserved juice

¼ cup red wine vinegar

¼ cup olive oil

¾ tsp Tabasco or other hot pepper sauce

½ tsp chili powder

1 Tbsp fresh lemon or lime juice

1 Tbsp chopped fresh cilantro

In a large bowl, combine the corn, beans, bell pepper, scallions, red onion, garlic, tomato, and jalapeño chile. Set aside.

To make the dressing, place the corn juice, vinegar, olive oil, Tabasco or pepper sauce, chili powder, lemon or lime juice, and cilantro in a jar with a tight-fitting lid. Tighten the lid and shake to mix well. Pour the dressing over the salad and stir to mix. Cover and refrigerate for at least 6 hours, or overnight. To serve, transfer the salad to a serving bowl and garnish with cilantro or red onion wedges.

ZESTY ASPARAGUS SALAD

Serves 4

The sharpness of the mustard in this salad accents the delicate flavor of the asparagus.

INGREDIENTS

1 lb asparagus

4–8 large lettuce leaves

1 hard-cooked egg, finely chopped for garnish

VINAIGRETTE

¼ cup canola or olive oil (not extra-virgin)

2 Tbsp red wine vinegar

1 tsp dry mustard, or 2 tsp Dijon-style mustard

¼ tsp black pepper

⅛ tsp salt

1 large garlic clove, crushed

2 Tbsp snipped fresh chives

Trim the ends of the asparagus. Soak the stalks in cold water to remove any dirt, then drain. Bring a large pan of water to a boil, add the asparagus, and cook for 5–7 minutes until tender-crisp. Alternatively, steam in a large covered pot with about ½-inch boiling salted water for 12–15 minutes. Remove each stalk with tongs, and rinse immediately under cold running water. Drain, wrap in paper towels, and chill in the refrigerator for about 2 hours.

To prepare the vinaigrette, place the ingredients in a jar with a tight-fitting lid, and shake until thoroughly blended. Refrigerate for 2 hours before using.

To serve the salad, arrange 1–2 lettuce leaves on each of four plates. Divide the chilled asparagus between the plates, and spoon 1 tablespoon of vinaigrette over each plate. Sprinkle the salads with the finely chopped egg, and serve.

RIGHT: ZESTY ASPARAGUS SALAD

CLASSICO ITALIANA

Serves 4

The freshest basil and the tastiest tomatoes are needed for this dish.

INGREDIENTS

4 large beefsteak tomatoes, thickly sliced

½ cup extra-virgin olive oil

2–3 Tbsp balsamic, tarragon, or herb vinegar

salt and freshly ground black pepper

12–16 large sprigs of fresh basil

Divide the tomato slices evenly among four salad plates. In a small bowl, whisk the olive oil and vinegar together, and season to taste. Arrange basil leaves on the tomatoes and drizzle with a little of the dressing. Serve the remaining dressing separately, along with extra salt and freshly ground black pepper.

FATTOUSH

Serves 4–6

This popular Lebanese salsa has pieces of crisply toasted pita bread added just before serving. This allows the pita to soak up some liquid without becoming soggy.

INGREDIENTS

1 cucumber, diced

1 large red bell pepper, cored, seeded, and diced

4 ripe tomatoes, diced

2½ oz full-flavored black olives

bunch of scallions, thickly sliced on the diagonal

2 Tbsp chopped fresh flat-leaf parsley

2 pita breads, toasted until crisp and golden

juice of ½ lemon

3 Tbsp olive oil

salt and freshly ground black pepper

Toss together the cucumber, pepper, tomatoes, olives, scallions, and parsley in a large bowl. Tear the pitas into bite-sized pieces and add to the cucumber mixture.

Whisk together the lemon juice, olive oil, and plenty of seasoning. Pour over the salad, toss well together and serve immediately.

PASTA-TOPPED MUSHROOMS

Serves 2–4

The topping can be made in advance and arranged on the mushrooms at the last minute. Serve it cold with a crisp leafy salad, or warm as an appetizer or accompaniment.

INGREDIENTS

¼ cup dried small stellette (star shape pasta)

dash of olive oil

4 large flat mushrooms

TOPPING

¼ cup butter

1 garlic clove, minced

½ yellow bell pepper, cored, seeded, and finely diced

½ orange bell pepper, cored, seeded, and finely diced

generous ¼ lb blue cheese (Stilton or Danish blue), crumbled

salt and freshly ground black pepper

2 Tbsp chopped fresh parsley

Bring a large saucepan of water to a boil, and add the stellette with the dash of olive oil. Cook for about 7 minutes, stirring occasionally, until tender. Drain and set the pasta aside.

Cut the stalks out of the mushrooms and discard. Wipe the mushrooms with paper towel. Arrange the mushrooms, gill side up, on a baking sheet and set aside. Preheat the broiler.

To make the topping, melt the butter in a skillet, and sauté the garlic. Add the peppers, and cook for a further 5–7 minutes. Stir in the cheese, and season. Add the parsley and stellette. Stir well.

Top each mushroom with an equal amount of pasta mixture, then place the baking sheet in the broiler for 2–5 minutes, or until the topping is lightly golden and the mushrooms are warmed through.

ROASTED BELL PEPPER SALSA

Serves 4

Remember to leave the bell peppers covered for five minutes after broiling as the gentle steam that results helps lift the skin away from the flesh.

INGREDIENTS

2 red bell peppers

2 yellow bell peppers

2 orange bell peppers

2 garlic cloves, finely chopped

2 ripe tomatoes, finely diced

2 Tbsp chopped fresh flat-leaf parsley

4 Tbsp extra-virgin olive oil

3 Tbsp balsamic vinegar

salt and freshly ground black pepper

Preheat the broiler to medium. Place all the peppers under the broiler for about 10 minutes, turning them frequently, until the skin is blackened and charred. Remove and cover with a dish towel and leave to cool for 5 minutes.

With the point of a sharp knife, pierce a hole in the bottom of each pepper and squeeze all the juice into a jug. Reserve the juice. Peel away the skin and discard, then cut the flesh into ¼-in wide slices.

Place the warm pepper strips in a serving bowl with the garlic, tomatoes, and parsley. Whisk together the bell pepper juices, olive oil, and balsamic vinegar, and season to taste. Pour over the bell peppers and toss together well. Serve while still warm, or cover and chill for up to 4 days.

ALL-PURPOSE DIPPING SAUCE

Serves 4

This incredibly versatile dipping sauce can be served with almost anything. Try it with fried or steamed cubes of tofu or soy bean curd, blanched vegetables, or small kabobs of broiled meat or poultry.

INGREDIENTS

4 Tbsp good quality soy sauce

2 Tbsp white wine vinegar

1 Tbsp sesame oil

1 tsp dark brown granulated sugar

1 tsp chili flakes

VARIATION

chopped fresh cilantro or basil

toasted sesame seeds

finely diced tomato

minced garlic clove

shredded cucumber

finely chopped fresh green chile

finely chopped scallions

Blend all the ingredients together well, with 1 tablespoon water.

Add any one or a combination of the alternative ingredients (see left) for a good variation of the All-purpose Dipping Sauce.

RIGHT: ROASTED BELL PEPPER SALSA

Dressings & Marinades

MINT AND TOMATO VINAIGRETTE

Makes about 1 cup

Poured over a warm pasta salad, or cooked cold chicken or turkey, this vinaigrette makes a tasty meal from simple ingredients. It is also good drizzled over avocado or zucchini salads, or served with fish such as tuna or salmon.

INGREDIENTS

scant ½ cup olive oil

1 tsp white wine vinegar

1½ tsp lime juice

1 garlic clove, finely chopped

1 scallion, finely chopped

3 well-flavored tomatoes

1 Tbsp chopped fresh mint

salt and freshly ground black pepper

Put all the ingredients except the tomatoes, seasoning, and mint, into a bowl and whisk together until well emulsified. Peel, seed, and chop the tomatoes. Stir the tomatoes and mint into the dressing, and season to taste.

HERB VINAIGRETTE

Makes about ½ cup

Either a single herb or a combination of herbs can be used in this traditional dressing, but choose ones that complement the salad ingredients. Make the dressing up to 12 hours in advance, but do not include the herbs until shortly before it is to be served.

INGREDIENTS

2 Tbsp white wine vinegar or lemon juice

salt and freshly ground black pepper

1 Tbsp Dijon-style mustard (optional)

6 Tbsp olive oil

2 Tbsp chopped fresh herbs

Put the vinegar or lemon juice, seasoning, and mustard, if used, into a bowl. Slowly pour in the oil in a thin, steady stream, whisking until the vinaigrette has emulsified and thickened. Taste for seasoning and herb flavor, and adjust if necessary.

PARSLEY AND LEMON DRESSING

Makes about ¾ cup

**If possible, make the dressing a few hours before it is needed and store it in a cool place.
Mix again before pouring over salads of romaine leaves and croutons.**

INGREDIENTS

⅔ cup virgin olive oil

2 Tbsp lemon juice

1 tsp shredded lemon zest

2 garlic cloves, finely chopped

2 tsp chopped parsley

1 tsp sherry vinegar

1½ Tbsp freshly shredded
Parmesan cheese

salt and freshly ground black pepper

Mix all the ingredients together until well emulsified. Store in a sealed container in a cool place until ready for use.

OREGANO AND ANCHOVY DRESSING

Makes scant 1 cup

This strong flavored dressing is better suited to broiled vegetables like eggplant, bell peppers, zucchini, and onions, with tomato or green salads, or broiled fish.

INGREDIENTS

3 oz canned anchovy fillets

a little milk

1 small garlic clove, minced

1½ Tbsp finely chopped fresh oregano

juice of 1 lemon

5 Tbsp virgin olive oil

1 tsp sun-dried tomatoes in oil, finely chopped

freshly ground black pepper

Soak the anchovy fillets in milk for 5 minutes, then drain. Put the anchovy fillets into a mortar with the garlic and herbs, and crush together with a pestle to make a smooth paste, slowly working in half of the lemon juice.

Beat in the oil a drop at a time until half has been added. Stir in the remaining lemon juice then slowly trickle in the remaining oil, beating constantly. Lightly blend in the sun-dried tomatoes and season with black pepper.

RIGHT: OREGANO AND ANCHOVY DRESSING

PESTO VINAIGRETTE

Makes generous 1 cup

Possibly one of the quickest to prepare vinaigrettes of them all, is also one of the most versatile. It complements nearly all vegetable salads (beet is the one exception), and is great with egg, shellfish, chicken, turkey, and beef salads.

INGREDIENTS

5–6 Tbsp white wine vinegar

4 tsp pesto sauce

⅔ cup olive oil

salt and freshly ground black pepper

Put 5 tablespoons of the vinegar and the pesto sauce into a bowl. Slowly pour in the oil, whisking until emulsified. Season to taste and add more vinegar if liked.

TOMATO AND BASIL DRESSING

Makes about 1¼ cups

A light, clean tasting dressing for fish and shellfish, pasta, egg, chicken, or avocado salads. The walnut oil enhances the flavor of the tomatoes, especially the sweet sun-ripened ones. If necessary, add a little sugar to balance the flavor of the walnut oil.

INGREDIENTS

1 Tbsp olive oil

2 Tbsp walnut oil

2 Tbsp white wine vinegar

1 Tbsp sherry vinegar

3 well-flavored tomatoes

18–20 basil leaves, chopped

dash of superfine sugar (optional)

salt and freshly ground black pepper

Pour the oils and vinegars into a bowl. Whisk together. Peel, seed, and finely chop the tomatoes then stir into the dressing with the basil. Add a little sugar if necessary, then season to taste.

TARRAGON AND SESAME DRESSING

Makes scant ½ cup

With its nutty taste, this dressing complements sliced, well flavored ripe tomatoes. In place of the sesame oil you can use walnut oil.

INGREDIENTS

4 tsp chopped fresh tarragon

1 Tbsp Dijon-style mustard

2 Tbsp lemon juice

2 Tbsp sesame oil

dash of granulated sugar (optional)

salt and freshly ground black pepper

Put all the ingredients into a bowl and whisk together. Make shortly before needed and leave in a cool place.

PARSLEY DRESSING

Makes about 1 cup

The flavor of parsley does not vary much from season to season, so this is a useful and welcome herb dressing for the winter, especially as it happily combines with winter vegetable salads.

INGREDIENTS

2 garlic cloves

¼ tsp fennel seeds

salt and freshly ground black pepper

leaves from a large bunch of parsley

about 2 Tbsp white or red wine vinegar

zest of 1 lime, finely shredded

¾ cup olive oil

3 scallions, finely chopped

1 tsp chopped fresh tarragon (optional)

Put the garlic, fennel seeds, and a dash of salt into a mortar or bowl. Crush together with a pestle or the end of a wooden spoon until reduced to a paste, adding a scant 2 tablespoons of the parsley toward the end of the process.

Stir in the vinegar and lime zest. Slowly trickle in the oil, whisking until well emulsified. Stir in the remaining parsley, and the scallions and tarragon, and season with black pepper to taste.

CHIVE AND LEMON VINAIGRETTE

Makes about ¾ cup

Use this dressing to make a delicious, light potato salad by tossing it with warm new potatoes and finely chopped scallions. Allow the salad to cool before serving.

INGREDIENTS

1 garlic clove	1½ tsp wholegrain mustard
salt	4 Tbsp virgin olive oil
4 Tbsp lemon juice	2 Tbsp chopped chives
zest of 1 lemon, finely shredded	freshly ground black pepper

Put the garlic and a dash of salt into a bowl. Crush together, then stir in the lemon juice and zest, and the mustard until smooth.

Slowly pour in the oil, whisking constantly, until well emulsified. Add the chives and season with pepper.

HERB, LEMON, AND CAPER DRESSING

Makes about 1¼ cups

This dressing goes well with shellfish, cucumber, zucchini, egg, or green salads and with broiled fish like salmon and firm-fleshed cod. It is particularly good with fish cakes.

INGREDIENTS

½ garlic clove
salt
4 Tbsp lemon juice
4 Tbsp capers, drained
2 Tbsp chopped chives
2 Tbsp chopped dill
⅔ cup olive oil
freshly ground black pepper

Put the garlic and a dash of salt into a mortar. Crush together with a pestle until reduced to a smooth paste.

Stir in the lemon juice, capers, and herbs. Slowly trickle in the oil, whisking until well emulsified. Season with black pepper.

RIGHT: CHIVE AND LEMON VINAIGRETTE

CILANTRO, CAPER, AND LIME DRESSING

Makes about 1 cup

Try tossing this piquant dressing with warm potato or celeriac, but allowing the dish to cool before serving. It is also wonderful poured over fried fish or Feta cheese.

INGREDIENTS

1 garlic clove, finely chopped

1½ tsp wholegrain mustard

finely shredded zest and juice of 2 limes

1 Tbsp white wine vinegar

4 Tbsp virgin olive oil

3–4 Tbsp capers, drained

3 Tbsp chopped fresh cilantro

freshly ground black pepper

Put the garlic, mustard, lime zest and juice, and vinegar into a bowl and mix together. Slowly pour in the oil, whisking constantly, until well emulsified. Stir in the capers and cilantro. Season with black pepper.

BASIL DRESSING

Makes about ¾ cup

Save this dressing for summer when fresh basil is at its prime. Use it to dress warm pasta, shellfish, potato, zucchini, egg, cheese, or green salads, and broiled vegetables.

INGREDIENTS

2 garlic cloves

leaves from 1 large bunch of basil

salt

1 Tbsp white wine vinegar

6 Tbsp virgin olive oil

2 Tbsp shredded Parmesan cheese

freshly ground black pepper

Put the garlic, basil leaves, dash of salt, and vinegar into a small blender. Mix briefly then, with the motor running, slowly pour in the oil until well emulsified.

Transfer to a bowl. Stir in the Parmesan cheese and season with black pepper.

HERB, GARLIC, AND MUSTARD DRESSING

Makes about 1 cup

This is a quite strongly flavored dressing so is best used for more robust salads such as Niçoise.

INGREDIENTS

1–2 garlic cloves

salt

leaves from 4–5 sprigs of thyme

leaves and fine stems from a small bunch of chervil

1 tsp Dijon-style mustard

¼ cup red wine vinegar

¾ cup olive oil

freshly ground black pepper

Put the garlic, a dash of salt, and herbs into a bowl. Crush together then stir in the mustard and the vinegar until smooth.

Slowly pour in the oil, whisking constantly, until well emulsified. Season with black pepper.

WHITE WINE MARINADE

Makes about 1¼ cups

Even though lighter than a red wine marinade, this marinade is robust enough for farmed pigeon and rabbit, young partridge and pheasant, lamb, chicken, turkey, and pork.

INGREDIENTS

2 Tbsp mild olive oil

1 shallot, finely chopped

1 carrot, finely chopped

2 juniper berries, crushed

2 black peppercorns, crushed

1 sprig of celery leaves, chopped

2 sprigs parsley

1 bay leaf, torn

1 sprig of thyme

1 slice of lemon

about 1¼ cups medium-bodied dry white wine

Put all the ingredients into a bowl and stir. If the meat is not covered by the marinade, add some more wine. There is no need to add more herbs, vegetables, or spices.

HERB MARINADE

Makes about ⅔ cup

This marinade can be used for meat, poultry, fish, or vegetables.

INGREDIENTS

4 Tbsp olive oil

2 Tbsp lemon or lime juice or
white wine vinegar

1 garlic clove, minced

4 Tbsp chopped fresh herbs

freshly ground black pepper

Mix all the ingredients together in a non-metallic bowl until thoroughly combined.

ORANGE AND HERB MARINADE

Makes about 1¼ cups

White wine adds a special flavor to this aromatic marinade and therefore to the foods marinated in it. Use it for pork, chicken, duck, and lamb.

INGREDIENTS

juice of 2 oranges

⅔ cup dry white wine

3 Tbsp olive oil

1 tsp chopped fresh marjoram

1 tsp chopped fresh thyme

1 tsp chopped fresh rosemary

1 garlic clove, minced

freshly ground black pepper

Put all the ingredients into a bowl and whisk together. Add extra orange juice and white wine, if necessary.

HOISIN SAUCE MARINADE

Makes about ¾ cup

Hoisin sauce is a thick, slightly sweet, smooth Chinese bean sauce with a mild garlic taste. This marinade adds a distinctive yet subtle flavor to chicken and pork.

INGREDIENTS

6 Tbsp hoisin sauce

4 Tbsp rice wine

2 Tbsp olive oil

2 tsp chopped fresh thyme

freshly ground
black pepper

Put all the ingredients into a bowl. Stir together. If you need more, make a double quantity, rather than diluting it.

WARM MINTED LEMON CREAM DRESSING

Makes about ¾ cup

To make this creamy dressing, simply stir all the ingredients together. This is the ideal dressing for young sweet peas, sugar snap peas, snow peas, baby carrots, and baby corn.

INGREDIENTS

4 Tbsp crème fraîche or plain, unsweetened yogurt

finely shredded zest and juice of ½ lemon

1 Tbsp finely chopped fresh mint

5 Tbsp unsweetened yogurt

salt and freshly ground black pepper

Put the 4 tablespoons crème fraîche or yogurt into a small saucepan and heat gently. Stir in the lemon zest and juice, and the mint.

When warmed through, stir in 5 tablespoons yogurt, taking care not to let the dressing overheat. Season to taste.

RIGHT: WARM MINTED LEMON CREAM DRESSING

VINEGAR FLAVORED WITH HERBES DE PROVENCE

Makes about 3 cups

Patience is the secret with this vinegar. You must resist the temptation to use it before the flavors have had a chance to develop.

INGREDIENTS

3 large sprigs of tarragon

3 large sprigs of thyme

3 sprigs of rosemary

4 bay leaves

pinch of fennel seeds

3 cups white wine vinegar

Lightly bruise the herbs and then pack them into a jar or bottle with a tight-fitting lid. Pour in the vinegar and seal the jar. Shake the jar and leave in a cool, dark place for 2–3 weeks, shaking the jar or bottle daily.

Strain the vinegar, pressing down well on the herbs. Taste the vinegar to see if the herb flavor is strong enough. If it is not, repeat the process. A fresh herb sprig can be added to the prepared vinegar, if desired.

SALMORIGLIO

Makes about 1¼ cups

In Sicily, salmoriglio is used as the marinade for fish kabobs that are to be broiled or barbecued. Sicilians believe that the only way to make a really good salmoriglio is to add seawater. In the absence of this ingredient, sea salt is used. This marinade can be served warm as a sauce to accompany a seafood dish.

INGREDIENTS

1 garlic clove

1 Tbsp finely chopped fresh parsley

1½ tsp chopped fresh oregano

about 1 tsp chopped fresh rosemary

sea salt

¾ cup virgin olive oil, warmed slightly

3 Tbsp hot water

about 4 Tbsp lemon juice

freshly ground black pepper

Put the garlic, herbs, and a dash of salt into a mortar or bowl and pound to a paste with a pestle or the end of a wooden spoon.

Pour the oil into a warm bowl then, using a fork, slowly pour in the hot water followed by the lemon juice, whisking constantly until well emulsified. Add the garlic and herb mixture, and black pepper to taste. Put the bowl over a saucepan of hot water and warm for 5 minutes, whisking occasionally. Let cool before using.

THAI-STYLE MARINADE

Makes about ¾ cup

Here, typical ingredients of the Thai cuisine produce a well flavored marinade that can be used with great success for broiled tuna, salmon, or swordfish steaks, with firm fleshed fish such as cod, and with chicken.

INGREDIENTS

2 garlic cloves, minced	2 Tbsp chopped mint
1 fresh green chile, seeded and finely chopped	½ in piece of fresh ginger, shredded
	¼ cup lime juice
2 Tbsp chopped cilantro	1 Tbsp fish sauce
2 Tbsp chopped basil	1 Tbsp sesame oil
	freshly ground black pepper

Put all the ingredients into a bowl. Stir together until well mixed.

To marinate large quantities of meat or tofu, make a double quantity of this marinade.

GREEN GODDESS DRESSING

Makes about 2 cups

Sour cream was not used in the original recipe for this dressing which was invented in the kitchens of the Palace Hotel, San Francisco. This hotel was destroyed in the earthquake of 1906, but this terrific dressing for fish, shellfish, and vegetable salads lives on.

INGREDIENTS

1 cup mayonnaise, homemade

or bottled

½ cup sour cream

1 garlic clove, finely chopped

3 anchovy fillets, finely chopped

4 Tbsp finely chopped fresh parsley

4 Tbsp finely chopped chives

1 Tbsp lemon juice

1 Tbsp tarragon vinegar

salt and freshly ground black pepper

HOMEMADE MAYONNAISE

2 egg yolks

1 tsp Dijon-style mustard

2 Tbsp white wine vinegar or

lemon juice

1¼ cups olive oil or equal amounts of

olive oil and sunflower oil

salt and freshly ground black pepper

To make the mayonnaise, put the egg yolks into a bowl and stir in half of the vinegar or lemon juice, and the mustard. Add the oil, drop by drop, whisking constantly. After about half of the oil has been incorporated the rest can be added more quickly but continue to whisk, until all the oil has been emulsified and the sauce is thick and shiny. Beat in the remaining vinegar or lemon juice and season.

To make the dressing, put the prepared mayonnaise and all other ingredients into a bowl and stir together until they are well combined.

PEPPERCORN, MUSTARD, AND PARSLEY MARINADE

Makes about 1 cup

A spicy mustard paste to spread liberally over thick lamb steaks and chops to give them a real lift.

INGREDIENTS

1 Tbsp green peppercorns, finely chopped

4 Tbsp wholegrain mustard

3 Tbsp chopped white and green parts of scallions

½ cup fresh bread crumbs

3 Tbsp chopped fresh parsley

¼ tsp cayenne pepper

1 Tbsp corn oil

Put the peppercorns, mustard, scallions, bread crumbs, parsley, and cayenne pepper into a bowl and stir together thoroughly. Stir in the oil a drop at a time to make a thick paste.

YOGURT AND MINT MARINADE

Makes about ½ cup

The mint in combination with yogurt produces a meltingly wonderful marinade for tender lamb kabobs, broiled lamb chops, and roast lamb. It can also be used successfully with chicken and turkey.

INGREDIENTS

6 Tbsp unsweetened Greek-style yogurt

1 garlic clove, minced

about 2 Tbsp chopped fresh mint

freshly ground black pepper

Stir all the ingredients together in a bowl until they are all thoroughly combined.

Pour the marinade over the meat, cover, and then chill for at least 2 hours.

HERB FLAVORINGS
& PRESERVES

MIXED PICKLE OF SUMMER VEGETABLES

Fills about seven 1 lb jars

Leave this light, crunchy, colorful pickle for at least six weeks before using so that it can mature. Once opened, it will keep for up to two weeks. Correctly stored and sealed, an unopened jar will keep for up to four months.

INGREDIENTS

1 small cauliflower, cut into small florets

8 oz French beans, topped, tailed, and cut into 1 in lengths

8 small carrots, thinly sliced

2 yellow bell peppers, cored, seeded, and cut into 1 in strips

2 red bell peppers, cored, seeded, and cut into 1 in strips

4 red or green chile peppers, cored, seeded, and very thinly sliced

16 scallions, cut into 1 in lengths

6–7 garlic cloves (one per jar), peeled

6–7 fresh dill sprigs or fennel sprigs (one per jar)

3½–4 cups white wine vinegar

⅓ cup salt

3½–4 cups water

Start by preparing the different vegetables; they need to be sliced and cut into quite small pieces so that they fit easily into the jar. Then prepare storage jars for the pickle; sterilize them and make sure they are cold and dry before use.

In a large bowl, mix the cauliflower, French beans, carrots, bell peppers, chile peppers, and scallions together. Then pack them into cold, sterilized jars, distributing the smaller quantities such as the chile peppers and scallions equally. Put 1 garlic clove and 1 dill sprig into each jar.

Pour the vinegar into a non-reactive saucepan, add the salt and water. Set the saucepan over a high heat and bring the contents to a boil. Remove from the heat and allow to cool slightly. Pour the vinegar solution over the vegetables and seal immediately.

CILANTRO AND MINT RELISH

Makes about 14 oz

With a beautiful, bright green color and a fresh, hot flavor, this relish is good with curries.

INGREDIENTS

½ cup chopped fresh cilantro

1 green chile pepper, seeded
and chopped

2 Tbsp freshly squeezed lemon juice

2 Tbsp water

¼ cup chopped fresh mint

2 tsp shredded fresh ginger root or
bottled ginger paste

⅓ tsp salt

6 Tbsp unsweetened yogurt

Put half of the cilantro into a food processor with the chile pepper, lemon juice, and water and blend to a purée. Add the mint, ginger, and salt and blend. Then add the remaining cilantro and blend again.

Put the yogurt into a bowl and mix in the herb paste. Chill.

MUSHROOMS PICKLED IN WHITE WINE

Fills about six 1 lb jars

Preserved in a light wine and vinegar pickle, these mildly spiced mushrooms retain all their succulence. Leave the pickled mushrooms for at least one week before using.

INGREDIENTS

3½–4 cups white wine vinegar

2 dried red chile peppers

2 blades mace

1 small piece dried root ginger, bruised

3 lb button mushrooms

2 Tbsp salt

1½ cups dry white wine, plus extra

6 thyme sprigs (one per jar, optional)

Pour the vinegar into a saucepan and add the chile peppers, mace, and ginger. Bring to a boil, lower the heat, and simmer, covered for 10 minutes. Allow to cool and then strain it.

Sprinkle the mushrooms with salt, leave for 30 minutes and drain. Put them into a saucepan over a low heat for about 3 minutes. Increase the heat and cook, stirring, for 5 minutes, until cooked.

Pour in the spiced vinegar and simmer for 10 minutes. Place in a plastic container. Cover and leave for 24 hours.

Strain the mushrooms, reserving the vinegar, and pack them into warm, sterilized jars. Measure the vinegar (about 1½ cups) and mix it with an equal quantity of dry white wine. Pour over the mushrooms. Add a thyme sprig, then seal the jars.

RED ONION RELISH

Fills about two 1 lb jars

Based on a Mexican recipe, this mild tasting, purple-red relish will add interest to casseroles and rice dishes. It may be eaten the day after preparation, but will keep for up to one month if correctly bottled. Once opened, it must be stored, covered, in a refrigerator and eaten within one week.

INGREDIENTS

1 lb red onions, thinly sliced

1 Tbsp salt

1 tsp dried oregano or marjoram

1¼ cups white wine vinegar

juice of ½ lemon

6 Tbsp water

Put the onions into a bowl and sprinkle with salt. Leave to stand for 30 minutes.

Pour boiling water over the onions and drain them immediately. Allow them to cool. When the onions are completely cold, pack them into cold, sterilized jars, adding a little of the oregano or marjoram to each jar.

In a bowl or jug, mix together the vinegar, lemon juice, and water and pour over the onion slices. Seal the jars immediately.

WALNUT AND CILANTRO RELISH

Makes about 1 cup

This rich walnut relish is a good accompaniment for curry dishes.

INGREDIENTS

1½ cups shelled whole walnuts

6 Tbsp chopped fresh cilantro

juice of ½ lemon

¼ tsp cayenne pepper

4 Tbsp unsweetened yogurt

Put all the walnuts into a food processor to finely chop them. Add all the remaining ingredients and work into a paste.

MUSHROOM RELISH

Fills 1 lb jar

Serve this relish immediately it is prepared, or store it in a refrigerator for two weeks in a covered container. If correctly bottled it can be kept, unopened, for up to three weeks.

INGREDIENTS

8 oz open mushrooms

1 medium onion, finely chopped

1 garlic clove, finely chopped

3 Tbsp olive or sunflower oil

6 Tbsp red wine vinegar

4 Tbsp chopped fresh parsley

¼ tsp whole black peppercorns, coarsely crushed

Very finely chop the mushrooms, preferably using a food processor. Heat the oil in a non-reactive saucepan over a low heat. Put in the onion and garlic and cook for about 3 minutes to soften them. Raise the heat to medium. Pour in the vinegar and bring it to a boil. Add the mushrooms, parsley, and peppercorns. Bring to a boil, lower the heat, and simmer, uncovered, for 10 minutes, or until the mushrooms are cooked through.

Either allow the relish to cool before serving, or spoon it while still hot into a warm, sterilized jar, and seal immediately.

LEMONS AND LIMES PICKLED IN OIL

Fills about four 1 lb jars

This unlikely combination of ingredients produces a bitter pickle that is surprisingly good with rich, spicy dishes. It is best to buy unwaxed or organically grown lemons and limes. Leave the pickle for three weeks before using. Unopened and correctly bottled it will keep for up to three months. Once opened, consume within a week.

INGREDIENTS

6 lemons

6 limes

4 Tbsp salt

2 tsp allspice (Jamaica pepper) berries

2 tsp cilantro seeds

4 bay leaves (one per jar)

8 dried chile peppers (two per jar)

3½–4 cups sunflower oil

Scrub the lemons and limes and slice them thinly. Put them into a colander and sprinkle them with salt. Set them aside for at least 24 hours, then rinse and drain them. Pack the citrus slices into cold sterilized jars, sprinkling a few allspice berries and cilantro seeds into each jar. Push one bay leaf and two dried chile peppers into each jar. Fill the jars with the oil and seal them up immediately.

THAI TOMATO SAUCE

Serves 6

Mouth-watering and moreish is the best description for this tomato-based accompaniment to fried appetizers, like spicy vegetable rolls or crab cakes. Any leftover sauce can be kept, covered, in a refrigerator for up to two days.

INGREDIENTS

3 large tomatoes, peeled, seeded, and roughly chopped

1 Tbsp sunflower oil

2 tsp sesame oil

1 Tbsp Tamarind Paste

handful fresh basil leaves

1 stalk fresh lemon grass

2 Tbsp dark soy sauce

1 tsp hot chili sauce

salt and freshly ground black pepper

TAMARIND PASTE

1 heaped Tbsp prepared tamarind pulp

3 Tbsp boiling water

To make Tamarind paste, beat together the Tamarind pulp and boiling water, then force the mixture through a fine non-metallic sieve to get a smooth sauce. Store in the refrigerator.

To make the sauce, place all the ingredients and the prepared Tamarind Paste in a saucepan, cover and simmer gently, stirring occasionally, for 45 minutes, until thick and pulpy. Strain the sauce through a fine non-metallic sieve and return to the rinsed-out pan. Season to taste and heat through. Serve this sauce while it is still hot.

CHIMICHURRI SALSA

Serves 6

**Popular in Argentina and Brazil, this onion, parsley, and chile salsa is simple to make.
It is traditionally served with plain broiled or barbecued meats.**

INGREDIENTS

*2 red onions or 4 purple shallots,
finely chopped*

*2 hot red chiles, seeded and
finely chopped*

1 large garlic clove, finely chopped

4 Tbsp chopped fresh parsley

2 Tbsp olive oil

freshly squeezed juice of 1 lemon

*salt and freshly ground
black pepper*

Place all the ingredients in a large bowl and toss together well. Season to taste, cover, and chill for 1–2 hours before serving.

BLACK OLIVE AND PLUM TOMATO SALSA

Serves 4

**For a delicious appetizer or light supper dish, place a slice of goat's cheese on a slice of fresh,
crusty French or Italian bread. Broil until the cheese bubbles and is golden in color.
Serve immediately with a large spoonful of this fragrant salsa.**

INGREDIENTS

6 plum tomatoes, roughly diced

1 cup black olives, left whole

6 scallions, thinly sliced

2 Tbsp olive oil

1 Tbsp balsamic vinegar

1 garlic clove, finely chopped

1 Tbsp chopped fresh basil

salt and freshly ground black pepper

Place the tomatoes and olives in a serving bowl and toss well together. Sprinkle over the scallions.

Whisk together the olive oil, balsamic vinegar, garlic, basil, and plenty of seasoning. Drizzle over the tomato, scallions, and olives, and serve immediately.

CAJUN SPICE RUB

Makes about 7 tablespoons

In addition to dried herbs and ground cumin, this spice rub also contains onion and garlic. It is perfect for all red meats. For an alternative taste, substitute dried basil, sage, or fennel for thyme and oregano.

INGREDIENTS

1 plump garlic clove
½ small onion, chopped
1 tsp dried thyme
1 tsp dried oregano

½ tsp ground cumin

½ tsp dry mustard powder

½ tsp freshly ground

black pepper

Put the garlic and onion into a mortar or small bowl and crush with a pestle or the end of a wooden spoon. Mix in the remaining ingredients.

SPICE RUB FOR MEAT

Makes about 7 tablespoons

Turn the simplest meat dish into something special with this aniseed flavored rub.

INGREDIENTS

1 tsp finely chopped fresh oregano

1 tsp fennel seeds, crushed

½ small garlic clove, finely chopped

1 Tbsp paprika pepper

½ tsp cayenne pepper

freshly ground black pepper

Put all the ingredients into a bowl and mix together to combine thoroughly.

Rub a generous amount onto both sides of the meat you are using.

ROAST GARLIC MAYONNAISE

Makes about 1½ cups

Roasting garlic softens its flavor and gives it a smoky taste which, in turn, adds an enticing flavor to the mayonnaise. For extra taste, add two mashed anchovy fillets to the mixture at the same time as the egg yolks are added.

INGREDIENTS

2 garlic bulbs, unpeeled

2 sprigs of thyme or rosemary

2 Tbsp olive oil

2 egg yolks

2–3 tsp lemon juice

1¼ cups virgin olive oil

salt and freshly ground black pepper

Preheat the oven to 350°F. Put each garlic bulb on a piece of wax paper. Add a thyme or rosemary sprig and trickle over 1 tablespoon of the olive oil. Fold up the wax paper to enclose the contents, sealing the edges together firmly. Place the bulbs on a baking sheet and bake for 35–40 minutes until the garlic is soft. Allow the garlic to cool slightly then gently squeeze the garlic cloves from their skins, into a bowl. Add the egg yolks and 1 teaspoon of the lemon juice. Beat hard.

Beat in olive oil drop by drop until half of the oil has been added. Add another 1 teaspoon of lemon juice then slowly trickle in the remaining oil, beating hard, constantly. Season and add more lemon juice, if necessary.

SPICE RUB FOR FISH

Makes about 9 tablespoons

The lemon, tarragon, and basil in this rub make it particularly suitable for fish such as tuna, salmon, and red mullet. However, it is also good used on chicken and is particularly popular at barbecue parties.

INGREDIENTS

2 tsp finely shredded lemon zest

1 tsp dried tarragon, finely chopped

1 tsp dried basil, chopped

½ small garlic clove, finely chopped

1 Tbsp paprika pepper

½ tsp cayenne pepper

freshly ground black pepper

Put all the ingredients into a bowl and stir together making sure all the herbs are combined well.

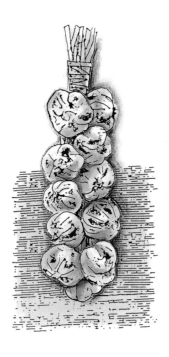

SPICE RUB FOR POULTRY

Makes about 7 tablespoons

**The strong herb flavors in this rub will even liven up deep-frozen chicken or turkey.
As this rub is quick and easy to prepare it makes a very good flavoring to spice
up a meal for busy people.**

INGREDIENTS

1 tsp dried tarragon, finely chopped

¾ tsp dried marjoram, finely chopped

¼ tsp dried thyme, finely chopped

¼ tsp dried sage, finely chopped

½ small garlic clove, finely chopped

1 Tbsp paprika pepper

½ tsp cayenne pepper

freshly ground black pepper

Put all the ingredients, making sure they are finely chopped first, into a bowl and mix together.

LIGHT HERB SAUCE

Makes about ¾ cup

**A simple, quick sauce that can be flavored with any herb. If you prefer a milder dressing, leave out the
shallot. Serve the dressing over green salads, warm new potatoes, vegetable salads, or warm white
beans.**

INGREDIENTS

*⅔ cup sour cream, thick yogurt or
unsweetened yogurt*

2 Tbsp chopped fresh herbs

1 tsp finely chopped shallot

*salt and freshly ground white or
black pepper*

Put the sour cream or yogurt, herbs, and shallots into a bowl. Stir together and season to taste.

Store in the refrigerator until ready to use.

GARLIC SPICE RUB

Makes about 5 tablespoons

This spice rub is especially effective on lamb and pork, but it can also be enjoyed with chicken and turkey. Garlic is such a universally enjoyed flavoring that this spice rub is ideal to use when feeding large numbers of people, at a dinner party or barbecue.

INGREDIENTS

1 tsp dried thyme

4 garlic cloves, finely chopped

1 dried bay leaf, crushed

6 black peppercorns, crushed

Put all the ingredients into a bowl and mix together until thoroughly combined.

Store in a sealed container in the refrigerator if you do not wish to use it immediately.

SAUCE VERTE

Makes 1½ cups

A favorite dressing for cold summer platters of salmon or poultry. The dressing also complements hard-cooked eggs and many boiled or steamed vegetables served cold.

INGREDIENTS

4 oz mixed herbs and leaves (sorrel, watercress, and spinach)

1½ cups bottled mayonnaise

Add the herbs and leaves to a saucepan of boiling water and boil for 30 seconds. Drain and rinse under cold running water. Drain well and squeeze dry. Chop finely or purée in a blender. Add the herbs and leaves to the mayonnaise. Cover and chill.

YOGURT AND CUCUMBER SAUCE

Makes about 1 cup

This is an extremely simple sauce to accompany meat-stuffed vegetables, such as bell peppers, zucchini, and eggplant. Mint or cilantro, as desired, lends real Middle Eastern flavor.

INGREDIENTS

1 garlic clove, minced

salt

1 cup Greek-style yogurt

1 large or 1½ small cucumbers, peeled, seeded, and shredded

1 Tbsp finely chopped fresh mint or cilantro

freshly ground black pepper

In a bowl, mash the garlic and about 1 teaspoon salt together. Stir in the yogurt, cucumber, and the mint or cilantro. Taste, season further to taste, stir again, and serve immediately or chill.

This sauce can be refrigerated for up to one week. It is not suitable for freezing.

PESTO SAUCE

Serves 4–6

Use this strong sauce in moderation in pasta dishes, or if added to other sauces or used as an ingredient in recipes. The texture of the pesto can be left relatively coarse or puréed until smooth.

INGREDIENTS

2 garlic cloves, minced

8 Tbsp chopped fresh basil

2 Tbsp chopped fresh parsley

scant ½ cup pine nuts

1 cup fresh shredded Parmesan cheese

⅔ cup extra-virgin olive oil

salt and freshly ground black pepper

Place all the ingredients in a blender or food processor, and blend to the desired texture.

Stir this classic Italian pesto sauce into freshly cooked pasta tossed in butter and freshly ground black pepper. Serve the dish immediately with additional shredded Parmesan cheese if desired and a fresh green salad.

INDEX